SOME LIKE IT HOT

Me, Marilyn and the Movie

Tony Curtis

With Mark A Vieira

Published by Virgin Books 2009

2 4 6 8 10 9 7 5 3 1

Copyright © Tony Curtis 2009

Published in the United States by John Wiley & Sons, Inc.,
Hoboken, New Jersey

Tony Curtis has asserted his right under the Copyright, Designs and Patents Act
1988 to be identified as the author of this work

Photo insert page 1, United Artists/Photofest; page 7 bottom, Photofest. All
other photos in text and insert courtesy of Tony Curtis.

Every reasonable effort has been made to contact copyright holders of
material reproduced in this book. If any have been overlooked inadvertently
the publisher would be glad to hear from them and make good in future
editions any errors or omissions brought to their attention.

First published in Great Britain in 2009 by
Virgin Books
Random House, 20 Vauxhall Bridge Road,
London SW1V 2SA

www.virginbooks.com
www.rbooks.co.uk

Addresses for companies within The Random House Group Limited
can be found at: www.randomhouse.co.uk/offices.htm

The Random House Group Limited Reg. No. 954009

A CIP catalogue record for this book
is available from the British Library

Hardback ISBN 9781905264964
Trade paperback ISBN 9780753522257

The Random House Group Limited supports The Forest
Stewardship Council (FSC), the leading international forest
certification organisation. All our titles that are printed on
Greenpeace approved FSC certified paper carry the FSC logo.
Our paper procurement policy can be found at
www.rbooks.co.uk/environment

Mixed Sources
Product group from well-managed
forests and other controlled sources
www.fsc.org Cert no. TT-COC-2139
© 1996 Forest Stewardship Council
FSC

Printed and bound in Great Britain by
CPI Mackays, Chatham ME5 8TD

To Marilyn, Jack, and Billy—I wish you were here

CONTENTS

CONTENTS

ACKNOWLEDGMENTS

Tony wishes to acknowledge and thank the following:

- My wife, Jill, who has the patience and love of a saint. She encouraged me to do this book, and I couldn't and wouldn't do any of this without her. I love her dearly.
- Everyone who worked on *Some Like It Hot*. Films are collaborative projects. Everyone involved is instrumental in making a film into a work of art. These folks did that and more. They made it one of the best loved in history.
- Billy Wilder, whose genius changed my life. And his loving and beautiful wife, Audrey, who supported Billy in so many ways and allowed his talent to thrive.
- Mark A. Vieira, who stepped into this project with the most gusto I've seen in a long time. He took control, did massive amounts of research to help my failing memory, and was a joy to work with. He worked his one typing finger to the bone, met the tight schedule we gave him, and told one hell of a story.
- Alan Nevins, whom I've come to admire and enjoy immensely. He conjured the idea for this book while we laughed together backstage at *The Bonnie Hunt Show*. I love his spirit and his guidance, and now I understand why he came so highly

recommended by my Hollywood peers. He's my agent and my friend. Thank you, handsome!

And last, but not least, all the girls in Sweet Sue's band. You know who you are and why I am thanking you. All my love to each and every one of you!

Mark wishes to acknowledge and thank the following:

- The following institutions, archives, and individuals: Dorinda Hartmann, assistant archivist at the Wisconsin Center for Film and Theater Research at the Wisconsin Historical Society; Ned Comstock of the Cinematic Arts Library of the University of Southern California; and Barbara Hall of the Margaret Herrick Library at the Fairbanks Center for Motion Picture Study.
- Research assistants Karie Bible and Jonathan Quiej.
- Research helpers and consultants Preston Ahearn, Jack Allen, Dan Auiler, Alison Castle, Paul Diamond, Warren G. Harris, Anthony Mattero, Mike Thomas, and George Zeno.
- Manuscript reviewers Howard Mandelbaum, Rex McGee, Harvey Stewart, P. R. Tooke, and George Zeno.
- My literary agent, Alan Nevins, of Renaissance Literary Agency, for his ongoing work on my behalf. I thank Stephen S. Power and Ellen Wright of John Wiley & Sons.
- Tony Curtis and Jill Curtis for inviting me to collaborate on the story of a lifetime.
- My parents. It was in a theater in East Oakland that my brother Guy and I saw the coming attractions for *Some Like It Hot*. Because we had signed the Legion of Decency pledge, my father told us, "Look at the Exit sign!" (And not at M.M.'s nude soufflé.) Thirty years later, I watched the film with my parents on public television. It was worth waiting for. I trust that they would approve of my involvement in this naughty project.

Introduction

My name is Tony Curtis. You know me. I'm an actor. I've made eighty-eight motion pictures. Some of them are fun. Some are great. Some are classics. I enjoy traveling to festivals and conventions with my lovely wife, Jill. We go to these events and I talk about my pictures. I sit at tables and sign autographs for fans. A lot of them are young people. They weren't born when I made those pictures. That's what's great about movies. They survive. If I'd been on Broadway in 1958 instead of in Hollywood, who would see my work now? But they do, whether it's in a theater or on cable TV or on DVD. Do you know the picture they ask me about the most? *Some Like It Hot*.

This movie is a classic, sure, but it's more than that. It's in its own category. It's become part of our culture. Look at the American Film Institute—it's given *Some Like It Hot* these ratings:

#22 Greatest Movie of All Time
#14 of the 100 Greatest Movies
#1 Funniest Movie

Some people say that *Some Like It Hot* is the funniest movie ever made. I don't know. All I know is that it gave me a chance to work with four comic geniuses: I. A. L. Diamond, Jack Lemmon,

Billy Wilder, and Marilyn Monroe. It gave me a chance to improve my craft.

I'd had some success already, but I had an ego. I wanted more. I wanted to be an outstanding movie actor. *Some Like It Hot* was my chance to show the world what I could do. I played three characters. I had scenes that encompassed action, light comedy, slapstick, and sex. When the movie came out, I felt I'd achieved something. So did Hollywood. After that, I was a major player. I was given roles that both accommodated my talent and stretched it. I'll always be grateful to *Some Like It Hot*. It has a special significance for me. It has a unique place in film history.

I've written about the making of *Some Like It Hot* in my previous books. I've shared anecdotes about it. Because of the limitations of space, I didn't really get into the story as fully as I would have liked. I had some amazing experiences making it. I have a story to tell. It's almost like the traditional three-act play: intrigue, irony, suspense, comedy, sex. Yeah, lots of that. And unforgettable characters. Saying things that have become legend. Things I hear as clearly now as when I first heard them:

"You're the handsomest kid in this town."

"I laughed so hard that I fell off the couch!"

"The audience, the people, they'll walk out in droves. It'll be a disaster."

"Let's go to the ladies room."

"Where's that bourbon?"

"I have never met anyone as utterly mean as Marilyn Monroe."

"Well, nobody's perfect."

Yes, there's a story to be told, with sights, sounds, words, and feelings. And I'm the one to tell it, even fifty years later. Why not fifty years later? I've learned a lot about life. I see these events from a different perspective. And although I've had my share of health problems in recent years, I remember *Some Like It Hot* clearly. I want to tell the story of its making as fully and vividly as possible. I don't believe this has been done. I know it hasn't been done by someone who was there. I can relate it like a story, from beginning to end. And to be sure that I've got all the details right, I've done some homework. I've checked my facts and dates in books and archives and with helpful friends. What you're reading is the definitive account of the making of *Some Like It Hot*. I'm taking you there, month by month, week by week, day by day.

Okay. Where do we start? Hollywood, 1958. But first, to put things in context, I'll tell you where I was born: New York, 1925. My father was a tailor . . .

Part I

The Project

1

In 1958 I was the happiest of fellows. I was turning thirty-three. I'd been in Hollywood for ten years. I'd done five hit movies in a row, quality titles like *Kings Go Forth*. Each one was a success, both critical and commercial. I was getting reviewed for my acting, not for my looks. Because of my track record, I was at the point where I could choose a project and choose a director.

I'd been married to Janet Leigh for seven years. She was also a star. We were the Golden Couple, the most glamorous, happily married young stars in Hollywood. We had a beautiful two-year-old daughter named Kelly. We were expecting another child. Each year we were becoming more successful. Both of us. Janet had started at Metro-Goldwyn-Mayer in 1947. She'd become a star almost overnight. I'd started at Universal in 1948. By 1950 I'd made the transition from contract player to star. I married Janet in 1951. By 1953 we were celebrities. In 1956 we formed our own company, Curtleigh Productions. We coproduced *Sweet Smell of Success*, *The Vikings*, and *The Defiant Ones*. These pictures gave me opportunities as an actor that I'd never have had under contract at Universal.

This was Hollywood in the late 1950s. Actors were tired of being slaves to studios, so they flexed their muscles and became producers. The same thing was happening with directors. This brings me to Billy Wilder. He'd written and directed pictures like *Double Indemnity, Sunset Boulevard,* and *Sabrina*, but he was still beholden to studio bosses. He wanted creative freedom, and he wanted more money. He'd made a lot of hits for Paramount. Were they grateful?

Billy had just finished *Stalag 17*, a film about a World War II prison camp. Its dialogue was being dubbed for release in Germany. Billy had no love for that country. He'd left it in 1933 to avoid persecution. His mother and two other relatives had died in the Holocaust. He'd made both *A Foreign Affair* and *Stalag 17* to comment on that. What did Paramount do? To pacify German exhibitors, it changed a German spy in *Stalag 17* to a Polish spy. Billy demanded a change and an apology. He got neither. He didn't even get the courtesy of a reply. He'd been with Paramount since 1937. He'd made something like ten hits for those fools. So he turned his back on them and found a better way to make pictures.

In May 1954, Billy signed with Allied Artists. People shook their heads and wondered why he'd go to a low-class outfit like that when he had deals with Warner Bros. and Twentieth Century-Fox. I remember Allied Artists was way out there on the unfashionable stretch of Sunset. (The Allied Lot is now KCET-TV, public television; and the neighborhood is Silver Lake, which is quite fashionable.) Allied had been Monogram Pictures, part of what we called Poverty Row. They made cheap pictures there. Universal didn't exactly make great art, but its movies were masterpieces compared to what came out of Allied Artists: *Texas Bad Man, The Weak and the Wicked, Killer Leopard*. You get the idea. So did its vice-president. His name was Harold Mirisch. He'd made a fortune in the Midwest, but not by producing movies. He'd made his bundle with the Theater Candy Company, supplying sweets to concession stands. Now he was in Hollywood, and he thought Allied Artists could do something better than a killer leopard. So he signed three big-time directors: John Huston, who'd done *The African Queen*; William Wyler, who'd done *Roman Holiday*; and Billy Wilder.

Billy's first picture with Allied was *Love in the Afternoon*. It starred Audrey Hepburn and Gary Cooper. Some people complained that Gary was too old to play opposite Audrey, but the picture did okay, except that Allied was short of financing, so it got nervous and sold the foreign distribution rights. As a result, *Love in the Afternoon* wasn't as big as it should have been. Billy did his next picture, *Witness for the Prosecution*, elsewhere. This one was a hit. Harold Mirisch didn't want to lose Billy, so he offered him what nobody else could: Freedom. Creative freedom. And profit, lots of it, from a profit-sharing setup. But this wasn't possible under the roof of Allied Artists, where *Attack of the Crab Monsters* was the thing.

In August 1957, Harold Mirisch formed a company with his two brothers. Harold became president, Walter became production chief, and Marvin became vice president and secretary-treasurer. The Mirisch Company set up shop at the Samuel Goldwyn studio in Hollywood. Mirisch wasn't a studio, though. It was an independent producing company. The idea was to avoid the pitfalls of studio overhead. It didn't have expensive acreage or a large staff. Whatever it needed, it could rent, including offices at Goldwyn. A filmmaker could get a better deal with Mirisch than with a studio.

Billy Wilder signed a two-picture deal with the Mirisch Company. It gave him approval of story, script, casting, direction, the right of final cut—and 25 percent of net profits. Even with the less-than-perfect performance of *Love in the Afternoon*, Billy Wilder was one of the world's most successful movie directors. I mean, who else was there? Alfred Hitchcock. Howard Hawks. John Ford. But those guys came from the days of silent pictures. Billy was relatively young. I think he was about fifty, but my God he didn't look it. He was wiry. Energetic. I don't think I ever saw him stand still. Not a guy given to repose. Always moving. Like his pictures.

In 1957, the Mirisch Company signed a twelve-picture deal to release through United Artists—UA. That was another comeback story. When I arrived in Hollywood, UA was on the rocks. Mary Pickford and Charles Chaplin owned it, but they couldn't get along so they weren't producing. They were just releasing and distributing. They had some quality releases—*Champion, D.O.A.*, *Home of the Brave*—but most of the films they handled were programmers, cheap movies made to fill the lower half of double bills. They were losing millions every year. In 1951, Pickford and Chaplin sold UA to two lawyers, Robert S. Benjamin and Arthur B. Krim. These guys saw the big studios staggering under their own weight, losing their theaters to court orders, and scared of television. The moment was there. Benjamin and Krim offered an alternative to independents. No overhead. Great distribution. And profit shares anywhere from 30 to 75 percent.

By 1957, UA had transformed the Hollywood landscape. More than a quarter of that year's releases were independent productions, including two of Billy Wilder's three movies. And two of mine. There's a point to all this history. What happened to me in 1958 couldn't have happened five years earlier, when I was doing only what Universal told me to. I would never have gotten the offer from Billy Wilder.

2

It was a fine day in autumn 1957. You know the kind—just after the rain. No smog. The trees turning. The San Gabriel Mountains, cool and blue in the distance. I was cruising through Beverly Hills in the car that my agent, Lew Wasserman, had gotten me, a silver Rolls-Royce convertible with black interior. It was one of those what-do-I-do days. Things weren't all that pleasant at home, so I thought I'd go out and buy a new pair of shoes. Nothing like self-indulgence when you're vaguely dissatisfied. I parked just below Wilshire, made sure to smile at people who recognized me, and started looking for the shoe store.

I was walking down Beverly Drive when a man put his hand on my arm. I stopped. He looked familiar: a stocky guy in his forties, wearing horn-rimmed glasses.

"You don't recognize me, do you?" he said. "I'm Harold Mirisch. I put up the money for *Beachhead*."

"Oh, yeah," I said. "Sorry. How are you?" *Beachhead* was a picture I'd done four years earlier in Hawaii.

"You know, Tony, in the first two months of release, we made back all our money." He paused. "Because of you."

"Thanks a lot," I said. "I appreciate hearing that."

"What are you doing today?"

"I was going into this store to buy a pair of shoes."

"Let me buy them for you."

"You're kidding. Any kind?"

"Any kind you want."

So we went in. I looked around and found a pair of Symphony shoes. Black alligator, the most expensive in the store. Harold paid for them. It was a nice gesture. And an entrée into his circle.

Harold Mirisch was known for his parties. They were not so much parties as they were screenings. Movie parties. Before the so-called Beverly Hills circuit, there were guys like Harold who had screening rooms and projectors in their homes. Not sixteen millimeter. Thirty-five millimeter. Wide screen. The real deal. And the parties were catered, of course. So Janet and I started going to Harold's movie parties. He lived on Lexington Road, behind the Beverly Hills Hotel. He'd just built the house. The house? It was a mansion. Must have cost a fortune.

I met Billy Wilder at one of these parties. No deep conversation, just hello and nice to see you again, and then on to another part of the room. As I say, I was a star, but not in Billy Wilder's part of the firmament. As far as I was concerned, he was way up there, beyond my reach, making pictures with legends like Tyrone Power and Marlene Dietrich. He was nice enough, but that's because he was a nice man, not because he thought I was important in the scheme of things.

Parties were very important in Hollywood. Very often my agent would make sure I was invited to a party because he thought something was in the air. Lew Wasserman had been my agent since 1950. His agency was part of Dr. Jules Stein's Music Corporation of America. Thanks to Lew and Julie, MCA had its finger in a lot of pies besides agenting: radio, music, TV production. It was Lew's idea to get actors like Jimmy Stewart to incorporate. That way they paid less tax and retained more power. When Lew took me on, he was already president of MCA. I owe a lot to that man. With all that he was doing to reshape Hollywood, he still found time for me. He made sure that Universal let me do outside pictures. He made sure that the projects I chose weren't too tough for me, that

I didn't have to carry them all by myself—until I was ready. In the meantime, it was his idea that I be a presence at parties.

Sometimes the party would be at a producer's house, like Jerry Wald's, or a studio head's, like Jack Warner's. Other times it would be on a soundstage. The studio would dress up a stage, maybe like a Paris street or a Hong Kong street. If it was Hong Kong, they'd hire "Oriental" extras to wear costumes and be part of this setting. Or they'd decorate an outdoor set on one of those big backlots. They didn't mind spending money like that. They had it to spend. Guys like me were making it for them.

I once got an engraved invitation that said, "Dear Tony: Join us for an end-of-the-picture soiree down by the lagoon." It was signed, "Gregory Peck." I drove to Twentieth, parked my car, and rode in one of those little golf carts out through the backlot to the party. On the way I saw some of the new sets Darryl Zanuck wanted to impress people with the sets he'd built for *The Egyptian* and *The King and I*. I have to admit that they were impressive compared to what Universal was putting up. Finally the cart dropped me off at the lagoon. There were all these people wearing South Sea Island costumes. Everybody would come to these parties and eat and drink and flirt—and make connections.

One day in early 1958, Harold called me up. He wanted me to come to a movie party. Okay. But there was something different about this one. "Come by fifteen minutes early," said Harold. "Billy Wilder's going to be here. He'd like to talk to you. Can you do that?" I calmly said yes, hung up, and then I got all excited. *Billy Wilder*. Up to that time—with a few exceptions—Universal contract guys were directing my movies. I'd finally gotten to the point where I could pick the director. But Billy Wilder? Why would he want to talk to me? I couldn't understand it. I tried to put it out of my mind until the day of the party.

Janet and I were living on San Ysidro Drive at that time, off Benedict Canyon. On the evening of the party, I jumped into my car and drove down Benedict Canyon, heading for Lexington Road. Coming down the canyon on the way to this meeting, I felt like I was going down the Yellow Brick Road. I was touched by the idea that Billy Wilder would consider talking to me. The man had won three Academy Awards. He'd been nominated for twelve. Everything he did was quality. I'd been hoping for another quality movie, something that was really worth doing. Maybe, just maybe he wanted me to work for him. Those were the thoughts that were going through my head as I came down the canyon. I've never forgotten that drive.

3

When I arrived at Harold Mirisch's house that evening, Billy Wilder was there with his wife, Audrey. He was talking with Harold. When Billy saw me, he excused himself and led me into a little room in another part of the house. He shut the door. We sat down. I was nervous. I thought to myself, Are we sitting alone in here because he doesn't want to be seen with me? My anxiety was for nothing. He immediately put me at ease, speaking in a soft German accent.

"Tony, I wanted to talk to you about a picture I'm going to make."

I took a breath and leaned forward.

"The story is this," said Billy. "There are two musicians. Friends. They witness a murder. The murderer recognizes them and chases them. To get away, the two men dress up as women. Then they join an all-woman band. But there's a beautiful girl singer. Both of our boys fall for her. Of course they can't admit that they are boys. There's our conflict. And there's our story." He paused. "Maybe you don't like it."

"No, no. I like it. I think it's great. And—"

"I want you to play one of the musicians. He's bass player. And a goofball."

"Okay!"

"I'm going to use Frank Sinatra for the other musician, the saxophonist," Billy said. "And Mitzi Gaynor as the singer." He paused. "You and I have the same agent."

"Lew Wasserman, yes."

"I'll talk to Lew. How does that sound to you?"

"Mr. Wilder—"

"Call me Billy."

"Okay, Billy. Listen, it's great. Now you're sure you want to use me?"

"You're the handsomest kid in this town. Who else am I going to use?"

I don't remember what film Harold ran that night. How could I even look at the screen? I wasn't in a theater seat. I was on a cloud. I was going to be in a Billy Wilder movie. There were actors who'd kill for this part. He wanted me.

As I later learned, this project had been in the works for some time. Billy had a fertile brain. He always had at least three projects percolating. There was something he wanted to do about a Coca-Cola executive. There was something he wanted to do with Bill Holden and Audrey Hepburn. And there was this thing with the musicians. He got the idea from a 1935 French film called *Fanfares of Love*. He couldn't find a print of that film, so Walter Mirisch found him a print of the 1951 German remake *Fanfaren der Liebe*. Billy knew the writers who'd cooked up the original story and worked on the remake: Michael Logan and Robert Thoeren. He liked the idea well enough to ask Walter Mirisch to buy the rights from the German production company. Walter's attorneys had to do some sleuthing to track down the owners of the rights, but they finally found them. What Billy liked about the movie wasn't the labored workings of the plot. It wasn't that clever. Two musicians can't find work during the depression, so they go from band to band, disguising themselves so they can get hired. One band is "all Negro," so the musicians wear blackface. One band is Gypsy, so they wear earrings. And the last band is all girls.

Fanfaren der Liebe was what you'd call literal minded. It showed all the stuff that these guys went through to disguise themselves. It's not all that interesting watching men shave their chests. And when one of the guys goes back to men's clothes in order to sneak out at night, the real girls see him sneaking into his friend's hotel room. The girls get the wrong idea and beat up the guy who's still in drag. And so forth and so on. Billy put up with all these contrivances because he knew there was something there, something he could use. Not just use—transform. That's what he did. He didn't do it alone, though.

For many years Billy Wilder had a writing partner named Charles Brackett. Starting in 1937, the two of them wrote screen-plays for other directors. They weren't always happy with the result. Their dialogue was changed on the set by directors and actors. Scenes were cut. There was nothing they could do about it except become producers or directors.

Billy wrote eight pictures with Brackett before he got to direct one. That was *The Major and the Minor* in 1942. It was a hit for them, for Ginger Rogers, and for Paramount. Brackett copro-duced their next picture, *Five Graves to Cairo*. Billy and Brackett went on for about seven years, turning them out. Not just mov-ies. Great movies. Hits. I heard they had a kind of stormy work-ing relationship and weren't friends outside the studio. Billy had a sharp tongue. Brackett came from old money. They would yell and throw telephone books at each other across their office. It was an unlikely partnership. But they made these incredible pic-tures. *Five Graves to Cairo. The Lost Weekend. A Foreign Affair.* Then, suddenly, Billy didn't want to work with Brackett anymore. It was in 1950, when they were writing *Sunset Boulevard.* One day as they were starting a session, Billy told Brackett that it was over. Brackett was shocked, especially when Billy went right to work without answering any questions. Brackett stayed shocked, but he signed the dissolution papers. He never learned what had gone wrong. Years later Billy would say only that the match didn't strike sparks on the matchbook any more. You wouldn't know it from looking at *Sunset Boulevard.*

For the next few years, Billy collaborated with a series of dif-ferent writers: Charles Lederer, Ernest Lehman, and Harry Kurnitz, among others. Billy didn't like to work alone, yet no collaborator lasted for more than one film. One night in 1955, he and Audrey went to a Writers Guild dinner. It had a revue written by various members. One skit impressed Billy. It was about trying to sell an idea to Sam Goldwyn. The skit was written by I. A. L. Diamond. Who?

His real name was Itek Dommnici, but when he was in high school he was a tri-state champion of the Interscholastic Algebra League, so he changed his name to I. A. L. Diamond and went to Columbia University. When Billy was a star director at Paramount, "Izzy" Diamond was a junior writer. By the mid-fifties, he had plenty of credits, but nothing was really happening for him.

Billy liked Izzy's sense of humor, so Walter Mirisch signed a contract for Izzy to collaborate on *Love in the Afternoon*. The script was a beauty. Billy had found a collaborator who was as skilled in the English language as Brackett was, and witty in his own New York way but more accommodating. As Billy and Izzy would say, a writing partnership is like a marriage. When I met them, they were making baby number two.

How do writers write? Some of them write at home. Some get up in the morning and drive to work. Billy lived in a penthouse apartment at 10375 Wilshire Boulevard in Westwood. Lots of directors had mansions in Brentwood or Bel Air or Beverly Hills. Billy liked Westwood, maybe because its proximity to UCLA made it feel like a college town—in the middle of L.A. He liked having a place with lots of light, because he owned so much art. Rouault, Matisse, Picasso. He would treat himself to a new painting when he finished a picture.

Every morning at nine, Billy would meet Izzy in their office at the Samuel Goldwyn studio, 1041 North Formosa Avenue, Hollywood. This was located at the corner of Santa Monica Boulevard and Formosa Avenue. It was a block long, but it was a small lot compared to Paramount on Melrose or MGM in Culver City. Goldwyn was at one time owned by Douglas Fairbanks and Mary Pickford, then by United Artists, and then by Sam Goldwyn. It's the Warner Hollywood studio now. In 1958 it was a friendly place to rent an office. Billy's company was named Ashton Productions (after a street in his neighborhood). I remember that his office was on the second floor of an old writers' building. It was spare, but like him, it had an old-world elegance. And original art on the walls.

Billy and Izzy weren't doing well with *Fanfares of Love*. They liked the hook of guys in drag acting like guys who weren't in drag. But they couldn't get past one basic question. Why would a guy dress in drag if he didn't absolutely have to? They were stuck. You have to understand that Billy had been in a band in Germany in the 1920s when it was wild and you would see guys in drag in nightclubs. It was no big deal to him. There'd been a handful of Hollywood films with that conceit. *Queen Christina* had Greta Garbo dressed as a young guy for a few scenes. She managed it because she was Garbo. *Sylvia Scarlett* had Katharine Hepburn dressed as a boy. It didn't do well. *Charley's Aunt* had Jack Benny dressed as an old lady. Harmless fun, you might say. Yeah. And a huge hit. But two young studs in drag? No. The 1950s idea of shocking was Mamie Eisenhower wearing a sleeveless dress at a White House reception. If this movie was going to have guys in drag, there'd better be a good reason. "Nothing less than the threat of death," said Billy. "They're gonna get killed if they don't disguise themselves."

Izzy suggested that the story not take place in the present. If it was a period film, the drag wouldn't be so outrageous. It would be part of a big, splashy setting. "When everybody's dress looks eccentric," reasoned Izzy, "somebody in drag looks no more peculiar than anyone else. No matter how many times *Charley's Aunt* is revived, it's always done in period." America was starting to feel nostalgic for the 1920s. Compared to the 1950s, the 1920s were wild. The Jazz Age. The Era of Wonderful Nonsense. The Charleston, flappers, raccoon coats, Prohibition, bathtub gin, gangsters. Billy liked the idea of putting the story in the 1920s. This was a good day's work, so they adjourned.

The next day Billy came in all jazzed up. "Iz," he said, "last night when I was driving home, I got it. The Twenties. Gangsters. The St. Valentine's Day Massacre. You know there was a guy who was killed who shouldn't have been there. Some society guy. A thrill seeker, hanging out with these hoodlums. So he got killed. And the main gangster that Al Capone wanted to kill didn't show up. Now think about that. Wrong guy. Wrong place. Wrong time. We take our musicians. We put them there. But they don't get killed. They see it. They're witnesses. That's the motivation for the drag."

That's how my character was born.

Part II

The People

4

You might ask why Billy Wilder wanted me for this project. Who was I in 1958? How did I get there? Where did I come from?

My father was born in the town of Matészalka in Hungary. His name was Emmanuel Schwartz. He apprenticed with a tailor and came to the United States in 1921, when he was still a young man. A year later, he married a girl name Helen Stein, also from Hungary. I was born Bernard Schwartz on June 3, 1925. I don't know where my parents met or what led to their getting married. They weren't the kind of people who cuddled you and told you stories. And they didn't want to relive the beginning of a marriage that wasn't happy.

An unhappy marriage usually causes somebody an unhappy childhood. It did for me and for my brother, Julius, who was born in 1929. My parents were always fighting about money. My father had a series of tailor shops in New York's East Side, in Brooklyn, and in the Bronx. The first one I remember was on Lexington Avenue. He cared about his work and seemed content in it. My mother wanted him to be more ambitious. He wasn't a businessman. It just wasn't in him. She complained. He resisted. They argued. They screamed. Nothing improved.

Eventually my mother started taking her frustration out on me. She acted like she was mad at me, like I'd done something wrong. Sometimes she'd come after me. She'd grab me and spin me around and beat me until she was spent, and for no reason. These episodes terrified me, but I couldn't tell my father about them. I wanted to spend time with him, and I didn't want to mess that up with controversy.

He would take me with him to the synagogue. It was Congregation B'nai Jehuda on East Seventy-eighth Street. We'd attend on the big holy days. I can still see my father, rocking to and fro, wearing a tallith and a yarmulke, holding a prayer book, droning prayers in Hebrew. I didn't care much for it, but it gave me the chance to be with him. Other than that, he was always working. That didn't help when the Great Depression came. The bottom fell out of our business and out of our lives. We were evicted from our building and our clothes were scattered on the sidewalk. We ended up as squatters in an abandoned tenement.

When things improved, we moved to the Bronx and, eventually, back to Manhattan. My father opened a shop. It had a snazzy sign over it in big letters: Schwartz Dry Cleaning and Pressing. In smaller letters was: One-Day Service. We lived in a red-brick apartment building on East Seventy-fifth. Would you believe the rent was twenty dollars a month? My father was bringing in about one hundred dollars a month. He didn't pay taxes. When we went out for dinner, it cost thirty-five cents—for the whole family. This was 1937, so I was just about twelve.

As if things weren't bad enough at home, they got worse at school.

"What's your name?"

"Schwartz. Bernard Schwartz."

"Oh, yeah. Jewish."

If I hadn't had to say my name, I could have passed for Italian, German, or any one of a dozen nationalities that lived in my neighborhood. But as soon as I said my name, they put me in that pigeonhole. And I was fair game. You've heard the names they called us, filthy, hateful names. I'm not going to dignify them by repeating them here. But I heard them all through school. The sad thing was that I thought I'd have some peace at school, a different environment, an escape from the stress of my home. No. I went from one battleground to another.

I spent a lot of time on the street, defending myself or just dodging bullies. I developed balance, speed, and a sense of timing. It's amazing what you can do when you have to. Self-preservation, I guess.

Some of it was just kid craziness, like jumping from the roof of one apartment building to another. But it was exciting, and it took my mind off the problems at home. Sometimes Julie would come along, but usually I didn't want him there because he might get hurt. Even with an age difference of four years, we were close. Looking back on my life at that time, I have to acknowledge that he was the only person in it that I really liked. He was a gentle little boy. I trusted him. He trusted me. But when I went out to play, I rarely took him with me. I was trying to find my own way through the world.

In 1938, when Julie was nine, he was hit by a truck. I lost him.

After this happened, I tried to cope with life the best I could. As you might expect, I had episodes of depression. I'd had these while Julie was alive, but after he died they got worse and came more often. I never knew when they'd occur. All of a sudden I would lose interest in everything around me. I'd sit in my room. I wouldn't move. I wouldn't answer the friends who wanted me to play stickball. I would just sit there, immobile. One way I tried to cope with depression was by drawing. While my parents were in the shop, I'd sit in a corner and draw with pencils or crayons or even with tailor's chalk on my father's brown wrapping paper. I copied things I saw, but when I realized that I could add things, I discovered the satisfaction of creating something. Drawing what I was seeing—or better yet, thinking—became a driving force in my life. I was proud of my drawings. I showed them to a buddy. He made fun of them. After that, he was no longer my buddy.

Another way I coped was by being rough, rowdy, and athletic. Not on a basketball court or a football field; on the streets of New York. I would climb the trestles of the el trains like I was Tarzan. I would jump from the roof of one apartment building to another, sometimes downhill. One time I misjudged and bounced off the side of another building. I cracked a few ribs. But my favorite stunt was really dangerous. I called it trolley hitching. I'd start on the sidewalk under the el. When the trolley was going about twenty miles an hour I'd run next to it, jump up, grab the window bar, and hang on. My timing was split-second. It had to be. I couldn't afford a mistake. It was artful, but I never thought of it as anything other than physical expression. I was an athlete. Just like the ones I saw in the movies. Doug Fairbanks. Errol Flynn. Ty Power.

My other way of coping was by going to movies. The theater I attended most often, which is to say constantly, was the Loew's Spooner on Southern Boulevard in the Bronx. I would go to the movies. And go. And I would sit there, watching these extraordinary stars, thirty-five feet high on the big screen, and wonder if they had problems. If they were human. Maybe they weren't. Maybe they were immortal. These were the fantasies I had. They helped me survive.

I had a friend in high school named Gene Singer. One day I turned to him and said, "I want to be an actor. How do I get to be an actor?"

"I have no idea," he answered. But a few days later he said he'd asked around. He was a member of the Young Men's Hebrew Association. He said there was some kind of acting group or something in the art department there. "Go see this lady," he said, giving me a name. "It won't cost anything." So I did, and although nothing came of it, I got to see another kind of world. It intrigued me.

I was seventeen now, and my parents had had another child, a boy named Robert. His birth didn't bring me closer to my family. If anything, it pushed me farther away. World War II had just started. I was underage, so I forged my mother's signature and joined the Navy. I was in for three years, serving most of it on submarine tenders. I didn't see any real action, but I saw guys my age come apart at the seams, and I saw guys get stabbed and blown to bits. I got through it.

When I came back to the Bronx, I decided to go to school. There was the GI Bill of Rights. When I found out I could use it to attend acting school, you would've thought I'd discovered gold. I was that high on the idea. So I enrolled at the Dramatic Workshop of the New School of Social Research. It was located at the President Theatre at 247 West Forty-eighth Street (not at the New School campus on Twelfth Street). Erwin Piscator was the distinguished producer-director who ran the workshop and instructed us. He was known as much for epic theater theories as for his coaching of actors. I was there for a year, along with people like Bea Arthur, Harry Belafonte, and Walter Matthau. Then I got cast in an off-Broadway production of Clifford Odets's *Golden Boy*, the story of a boxer who wants to be a violinist. I got the lead. Somebody important came to see this play at the Cherry Lane Theatre. All of a sudden I got a call from a talent scout asking if I could take a plane trip to Hollywood, all expenses paid. I could.

On June 1, 1948, I was in Hollywood making a screen test for Universal-International Pictures. A week later I was signing a contract. It was the traditional seven-year contract with options every six months. I'd be attending dramatic classes at the studio while it spent time and money to groom me. If it worked out, I'd be a featured player. If not, well, there are a lot of those folks in L.A. They're called never-was-beens or Hollywood footnotes. I couldn't think about that. I was determined to make good.

Within a few months I was cast in a Burt Lancaster picture called *Criss Cross*. I had a two-minute scene in which I danced with Yvonne De Carlo. Just to show you how these things work, the studio started getting letters asking who the kid with the beautiful hair was. He was Bernie Schwartz when he arrived in Hollywood. By mid-1949 he was Anthony Curtis. And he was on his way.

5

Billy Wilder loved jazz. When he was a teenager in Vienna, he learned English by repeating the lyrics of American jazz records. Some of the first records he bought were by Paul Whiteman and His Orchestra. Whiteman's were among the first million-selling records. I remember hearing "Three O'clock in the Morning" and "Valencia" come out of neighbors' windows when I was a kid.

When Billy was nineteen, he was working as a reporter for the Viennese newspaper *Die Stunde*. One article he wrote was about the Lawrence Tiller Girls, an all-female band from Manchester, England. It was a nice assignment for a horny young guy. There were sixteen girls. They delighted his eye and tickled his funny bone.

"Do you believe in love at first sight?" asked one girl.

"If I'm looking at you, yes!" answered another.

"Who's Bernard Shaw?" asked a third girl. "I don't know him."

"Oh! I know *Hamlet*. It's a good piece."

"Oh, yes! Why doesn't this Shakespeare guy write musical shows?"

Billy never said if he got to first base with any of those girls.

A year later, in 1926, Paul Whiteman went to Vienna on tour. Billy made himself conspicuous—and indispensable—to Whiteman. Billy talked to him about jazz in broken English. A Whiteman violinist named Matty Malneck translated.

Billy was a bright kid, and ambitious. His articles about Whiteman were so well written that Whiteman took him to Berlin with the tour. That was the city where Billy's filmmaking began. You can see the part that jazz played in Billy's life.

In March 1958, when he and Izzy Diamond were working on their new project, *Fanfares of Love*, jazz became part of it. In the 1920s, popular songs and jazz flourished side by side. You could buy a straightforward rendition of a song like "Indiana." This was "sweet music," like you'd hear from a hotel dance orchestra. But you could also buy a jazz version. This was "hot," like you'd hear from Fletcher Henderson. And they were totally different. This concept was important to our movie. A person can be more than one thing, depending on the time, the place, whatever. Sweet or hot.

Billy changed the title from *Fanfares of Love* to *Some Like It Hot*. Izzy loved the nursery rhyme that ends with "Some like it in the pot / Nine days old." He really wanted to use the phrase "Some like it hot" from that rhyme for the film's title. It spoke to the music, the era, everything. It had been used before. A 1939 Paramount film, one of Bob Hope's first, was called *Some*

Like It Hot. There was an industry rule that prevented people from using the title of a copyrighted film. Walter Mirisch asked Lew Wasserman about this. It turned out that MCA was buying all Paramount films made before 1950 so it could lease them to local TV stations. Hollywood snickered at Lew for spending $50 million on old films. Lew had the last laugh. Putting these films on the *Late Show* sold millions in advertising, and he made his money back in spades. Anyway, Billy had to wait for the MCA-Paramount sale to close before Walter could clear the title *Some Like It Hot*. It took so long that at one point they considered an alternate title, *Not Tonight, Josephine*. But they held on to *Some Like It Hot*. The writing continued, and, with it, the casting.

Before Billy approached me, he'd considered Bob Hope and Danny Kaye for the two musicians. They'd both done drag before and were as funny as you'd expect. But a whole film? And they were a little long in the tooth to play young musicians. Let's face it: the idea of two guys in drag standing next to real women and not being detected was going to require the "willing suspension of disbelief" you read about in school. So the guys in drag had to be on the young side. I was thirty-two.

Walter Mirisch told Billy that the project needed a very big star. Billy approached Tony Perkins, but he was already signed for an Audrey Hepburn picture. When Billy talked to me at Harold Mirisch's, he thought that Frank Sinatra was going to do it. He'd gone to Palm Springs to pitch Sinatra the idea and thought Sinatra liked it. Billy made a lunch date with him in Beverly Hills to work out the details. Sinatra didn't bother to show up. Of course he was one of the most powerful men in the industry, so he could get away with that, but I'm sure it hurt Billy's pride. It had to. Billy made the best of it, and he later conceded that he could never have worked with Sinatra. "I'm afraid," said Billy "that he would have run off after the first take. 'Bye-bye, kid,' Frank would say. 'That's it. I'm going. I've got to see a chick.' That would drive me crazy." It looked like Sinatra was out. But UA still wanted a big star.

Billy thought about the character of the girl singer, Stella Kowalczyk. (Her name was later changed to Sugar Kowalczyk, singing under the stage name of Sugar Cane. The name was spelled "Cane" in our scripts, but changed to "Kane" before the premiere.)

Mitzi Gaynor was being considered for the part of Sugar. I thought that Mitzi was a major talent. She'd sparkled in *South Pacific*. But was she strong enough for this part? Sugar was pivotal to the story, but she wasn't as individual as either of the musicians. Jerry, the bass player, was earnest, adaptable, and wacky. Joe, the saxophone player, was a sexy, risk-taking skirt chaser. The friendship between these two guys was going to make the story. By comparison, Sugar was a little vague, which made Billy think. If Sugar was the weakest part, he needed to give it the strongest casting.

Now who was the biggest star they could get? Elizabeth Taylor? She'd just been widowed. Audrey Hepburn? Not right for a band vocalist. What about Marilyn Monroe? You'd better believe that the Mirisches liked *that* idea. Of course it had its drawbacks. Marilyn hadn't made a picture in two years. She didn't want to play any more "dumb blondes." Billy had directed her in *The Seven Year Itch*. She had great comic timing, but she had no concept of time. Stage fright and insecurity made her constantly late. When she finally arrived, she was unpredictable. "She had trouble concentrating," Billy said. "There was always something bothering her. Directing her was like pulling teeth." *The Seven Year Itch* made $8 million in 1955, but Billy said, "I'll never work with Monroe again."

The UA bosses were adamant. Billy had to sign a big star or he'd lose *Some Like It Hot*. There wasn't much hope that Sinatra would change his mind. Then Billy got a letter from Marilyn. He almost fell over. After the problems they'd had on *Seven Year Itch*, she was writing to tell him how much she'd enjoyed it and how very much she wanted to work with him again. What? He had to think about this. Oh, boy, did he. "Marilyn wanted the part," he recalled. "So we had to have Marilyn. We opened every door to get Marilyn."

Years later, he explained why he decided to work with her a second time. "When you got her to the studio on a good day," said

Billy, "she was remarkable. She had a quality that no one else ever had on the screen, except Garbo. No one. She was a kind of real image, beyond mere photography. She looked on the screen as if you could reach out and touch her."

On March 17, Billy wrote to Marilyn at the New York apartment she shared with her husband, the playwright Arthur Miller. Billy thanked her for her letter and enclosed a two-page treatment of the *Some Like It Hot* story. He was at his most persuasive in his letter:

> As one Arthur Miller will substantiate, nothing is more frustrating for a dramatist than to expose the bare bones of something he is working on. However, the script is only partly written, and since time seems to be of the essence, I would rather take the risk of sending this cold-blooded outline than of losing you altogether. You have to give me enough credit to assume that the piece, skimpy as it may sound in synopsis, will be written on the highest level, and that the characters will emerge live and three-dimensional. It has always been my theory that a story should be as simple and graphic as possible, to give oneself enough leeway to explore the characters fully, and develop the situations in depth. Don't be misled into thinking that this story is going to be treated as a farce—because unless some real emotion emerges from all this comedy, we will have failed.

Billy went on to tell the story in which Stella, the vocalist in an all-girl band, loses her heart to a saxophone player whom she has thought to be a girl. Billy mentioned Sinatra as a possible costar, and support from Edward G. Robinson, George Raft, James Cagney, and Paul Muni, plus the nostalgic appeal of Jazz Age songs that Marilyn could sing. Billy concluded his letter on a surprisingly straightforward note. "By all means," he wrote, "keep in mind that I'm dying to work with you again. Oh, yes—we want to get going on the picture sometime this summer—like about July 15."

The Mirisches were primed. They were still hoping for Sinatra, too. They figured $200,000 for him, $200,000 for Marilyn, plus a negotiable percentage of the gross. Billy waited for Marilyn to read the treatment. He heard nothing. He didn't press her. In late March he told Arthur Krim of United Artists that shooting could start in July—with Sinatra, Marilyn, and me.

There were rumors going around, so I called Billy. He was glad to hear from me. "Tony, we're putting it together," he said. "It's going to be you, Frank Sinatra, and Marilyn. And for the gangsters, we're getting Eddie Robinson and George Raft." After Billy said Marilyn's name, I didn't hear much. A lot of feelings were welling up inside me.

6

I've got a rich memory bank. It's bursting with treasures. Almost anything can open it up. A sound, a song, a scent, and memories come pouring out. So it was when Billy said Marilyn's name. After I hung up the phone, I wasn't in a den on San Ysidro in March 1958. I was in a garden on Sycamore Avenue in 1950. Sycamore House was my first residence in Hollywood. It was a rooming house for aspiring actors located on Sycamore Avenue, just below Franklin, and it was prettier than you might think: lots of trees and a garden and a pool, even though the pool was never cleaned. It was filled with leaves. But the feeling of the place was nice, very different from New York. There was one drawback, however. It was like the Studio Club on Lodi Place, where the young actresses lived. You could not invite anyone up to your room. If you wanted to go courting, you had to make other arrangements.

I wanted to. There were beautiful girls everywhere, popping out of doorways, falling out of pepper trees, breezing by in convertibles. And not just actresses. Every girl was beautiful, even the ones who rode bicycles from stage to stage and office to office at Universal, delivering scripts. I'd watch them as they breezed by. If one of them gave me a look, letting me know she was interested, I'd show my interest right back. I was still the brash kid from New York, shy and unsure, but I was trying to find myself.

I found my stage name in the one and only book that I read while I was in the Navy, Hervey Allen's *Anthony Adverse*. I'd seen the picture with Fredric March years earlier. I told a casting director that I wanted to call myself Anthony Adverse. "No," he shook his head. "The picture's being reissued. You'll look silly." I kept the Anthony. I had a relative named Janush Kertiz. Nice guy. Kertiz is a common Hungarian name. I modified it to Curtis. I thought to myself, *Tony Curtis*—what a perfect name that is, just a little mysterious. Universal agreed, and I became Anthony Curtis.

I first saw my new name in the papers on February 28, 1949. It was an article in the *Los Angeles Times* about the third picture I'd made, *City Across the River*. The article said that because of my work in the picture, Universal was going to give me a star rating. Wishful thinking perhaps, but I kept working, and my name kept appearing in the papers. And I kept getting cast.

The first time I was called Tony Curtis in print was in August 1950. Hedda Hopper, the famous gossip columnist, had been giving me coverage as Anthony. Suddenly she decided to use the name I preferred. Still, it wasn't until the release of *Kansas Raiders* in November 1950 that I was billed as Tony Curtis. But I was on my way.

And the girls knew it. I had lots of experiences. In those days I never knew what would happen when I went out with a girl. Sometimes we'd just neck, and sometimes things would lead to sex. I was fine with whatever happened. I was happy if they seemed to like me. One girl lived in a house that had a porch. We'd be out there 'til all hours kissing, but no more. That was it. Maybe if I had pushed for it, we could have had a romance, but I wasn't ready for that, at least not with her. I didn't want to lose out on all those others.

I was twenty-five and having so much fun that I couldn't believe it. To convince myself it was really happening, I made entries in a journal. I'd always liked putting my thoughts down on paper. Sometimes I wrote poems. In 1950 I was keeping a coded journal, recording the experiences I was having with the girls I was meeting.

It helped that I was driving a convertible. I'd had to buy three before I got a good one. The first one I got from a used car lot on Lankershim Boulevard. It was a dark green 1935 Chevy. The odometer was stuck at 183,000 miles, and there was a hole in the floor. The second one was a maroon Mercury. The third one was the charm. It was a light green Buick with white sidewall tires and Dynaflow Drive, which was a fancy name for an inefficient kind of automatic transmission. Looking back on it, I can see how L.A. that car was. I loved to cruise onto the Universal lot in it and park where everyone could see it. One day I was strolling by the studio guard post near the gate. The guard called me over.

"Did you see that girl?"

"Yeah," I answered. "I saw her."

Who hadn't? She was breathtaking. She was wearing a filmy blouse, and you could see her bra through it. When she walked down the street next to the Writers Building, heads leaned out of screen doors at crazy angles. Her beauty made her look unapproachable, but her smile sent a different message. She and I looked about the same age, but I later found out that she was a year younger. We had almost the same birthday. Mine was June 3. Hers was June 1.

"She didn't drive in," the guard said. "Be down here in twenty minutes."

I pulled up in my convertible, ready. And there she came, right on schedule. I got out and walked up to her.

"Hi. My name is Tony."

"My name is Marilyn."

"I'm driving into town," I said. "Can I give you a lift?"

She paused and looked at me for a minute. "Okay."

We walked to my car and I opened the door for her. I got behind the wheel, drove out the gate, and turned left, heading for Hollywood. I angled the rearview mirror a little so I could see her face. To my surprise she winked at me. We laughed. Nice.

There was something about having her in the car with me like that. Something extraordinary. She had an aura of sweetness and warmth. But as we made small talk, I felt something else. Heat. Sexual heat. I'd never felt anything like it. I remember exactly how she looked, with kind of reddish hair pulled back in a pony-tail. She wasn't wearing a lot of makeup like girls did then, just a little lipstick and mascara. It was a summer outfit she had on, and it lay on her body in just the right way. I could make out the out-line of her thighs, her back, and her breasts. Maybe it was goofy, but I fixated on her arms. They were beautifully shaped.

Now that I think of that day in my car, it seems quaint. Two kids, both aspiring to be movie stars. I'd gotten my break. She was waiting for hers. After a while, we didn't talk. We just rode along. I dropped her at a hotel where she was staying. It was the Beverly Carlton, a new hotel on Olympic Boulevard and Canon Drive. I thought it was kind of pretentious. She thanked me for the ride. I asked her if I could call her.

"If you like," she answered and wrote down her number on a piece of scratch paper. Then she got out, smiled, and walked into the building.

For the next few days I kept thinking about her, about her arms, and how she looked at me in the mirror. To tell you the truth, I couldn't think of anything else. But I didn't dare call. Not that soon. I didn't want to look desperate, and besides, a girl who looked like that had to be taken. For all I knew she was married. I hadn't seen a ring, though. Anyway, a week passed. I called her. "Hi, it's me, Tony, from Universal. Would you like to go out to dinner?"

A few nights later I picked up Marilyn at her hotel. I didn't ask why she was living there. I think she appreciated that. We drove to a restaurant on the Sunset Strip, the Villa Nova. We enjoyed the food and we chatted, avoiding anything serious. Before I took her home, we went for a spin on Sunset. It was an elegant street then. We had a fairly good time, which meant that there would be a second date. There was. It took place at a swanky club called the Mocambo. When we walked in, heads turned. Why not? We were a couple of healthy young animals. I was in a white linen suit and Marilyn was

in a flowered dress. She hadn't yet got that knockout look, but make
no mistake, she was fabulous. It was a weeknight, so the club wasn't
crowded. But Marilyn kept looking around, as if she were expecting
to see someone—or be seen by someone.

I wasn't aware of the tangled involvements Marilyn had, even
this early. She was being privately sponsored by Joseph Schenck.
(He was one of the original Hollywood moguls, the founder of
Twentieth Century–Fox, and in his seventies.) She was being
tutored by a drama coach, Natasha Lytess, who had an unre-
quited crush on her. She was being pursued by a voice coach and
composer named Fred Karger. She was represented by an agent
named Johnny Hyde, who was also infatuated with her. All these
individuals were older by at least twenty years. What was she
looking for? A patron? A protector? A parent? Maybe so. When
I later heard about her background, I felt that here was someone
whose childhood was more fucked up than mine.

Marilyn's mother was kind of a floozy. She worked as a negative cutter at a film lab in Hollywood. That was the first strike.
A lot of those broads were drunks. She couldn't raise Marilyn, so
she put her in a foster home until she was seven. Poor Marilyn
thought those were her real parents. Then her mother took her
back just before having a breakdown and being put in a loony
ward. Marilyn went through two more homes. One of them was
with her mom's friend, a character who brainwashed Marilyn to
think that she was going to be the next Jean Harlow. What a role
model for a frightened kid. But Marilyn bought it.

After marrying some young guy just to get away from the series
of foster homes, Marilyn went to work at a wartime factory. And
that's where it started. A photographer was doing a piece on Rosie
the Riveter types and saw how well Marilyn photographed. The
next thing you know, she was modeling. Twentieth signed her and
lost her. Columbia did the same thing. Then she started meeting
the Svengalis. When I met her, she was on the verge of stardom,
but not there. And she knew it.

During our dates we'd talk about the movie business. Marilyn
wanted to know about the people I'd met, how I'd met them, how
I'd handled myself, everything. When I related what I was going

through, she listened attentively, but when I asked about her, she didn't reciprocate. I didn't push her to open up. I knew better.

Marilyn was abstract. She didn't read the papers. She didn't watch newsreels. She was unrelated to what was going on in the world. Even as early as that, everyone around her was trying to get to her. But there was no way to get to her. There was no way in.

"Would you like some ice cream, Marilyn?"

"No."

"Don't you like ice cream?"

"I didn't like my mother."

What did that mean? That's how she talked sometimes, in non sequiturs. In her own language. You couldn't understand her. You couldn't get to her. Because she didn't want to be gotten to. And at that point, it didn't really matter. I was fascinated. I didn't need to take her apart and put her back together again. I just wanted to be close to her. But I couldn't bring her to Sycamore House. And I couldn't go to her hotel, which had the same kind of rules as the Studio Club. After our dinner dates, we'd drive to the beach, sit in the convertible, and watch the waves. We'd neck a little, but I always returned Marilyn to her hotel.

I was friends with the actor Howard Duff, who'd gone from being a radio star on *The Adventures of Sam Spade* to being a movie star in *The Naked City*. Howard had a beach house outside Malibu. He was a generous guy. "Use the house," he said. "I'm only there on the weekends." That was all I needed to hear. I called Marilyn. She agreed to go to the beach; that was all I prepared her for.

I picked her up at the Beverly Carlton. We headed out the Pacific Coast Highway and had dinner at a drive-in restaurant that served not only hamburgers, but also steaks and cocktails. By this time, the sun was setting. Even though I considered myself experienced with girls, I was feeling a bit nervous. I didn't want to look obvious, like I was taking her to the beach just to lie with her. This was a girl I didn't want to offend. We spread blankets on the sand. It was sweet. We just talked. She wanted to know more about me. I told her I had an actor friend who said we could use his place some time. She was open to the notion, so we went there.

Howard's beach house was a kind of bungalow. It was small and cozy with a fireplace and a little bar. There were bottles of whiskey and vodka. I offered Marilyn a drink, but I didn't really know much about mixology. She could see that, so she helped me make Scotch and sodas. We sipped them a little politely, it seemed, and then she started to talk about herself.

When she was a child, her mother had gotten ill. She never mentioned a father. She'd had various names. She'd been through a lot. I felt for her. It sounded like her life had improved in some respects but still wasn't that fulfilling. There was a lot of need there. She thought she could fill it by becoming a movie star. That was her overriding concern, it seemed to me, maybe because it was mine, too. There was a lull in the conversation. Then we started to kiss. We fondled each other a little while. That was the extent of it. I drove her home and went back to Sycamore. The next few times I called to make a date, she told me she was busy.

I was disappointed. I liked Marilyn. I enjoyed her company. If she was a little odd, that was okay. So was I. We were both trying to project self-confidence. It was just an act. Inside, we weren't comfortable. We were constantly worrying about what people thought of us. We hadn't found peace of mind, and we didn't know how to go about it. We were scared. I guess when you're in your twenties, that's how it is. You've got an adult body, but you're trying to make it work with a kid's emotions. With Marilyn and me, it was worse. Our kid emotions didn't even work. We'd been treated too poorly. I guess she sensed that about me. Maybe that's why she pulled away from me at this point. After a while, though, she called me and asked how I was doing.

We met for lunch at the Twentieth Century–Fox commissary. If you had a contract with one studio, you could eat at any studio commissary in town. I particularly liked eating at MGM, where I'd had some coaching. One day at the counter I met Judy Garland, just like that. She couldn't have been nicer. When I went on the date with Marilyn, people's heads swiveled. And this was in the commissary, where you saw nothing but gorgeous people. She had something, no doubt. I wondered how it made her feel to turn heads wherever she went.

I asked Howard Duff about using his house again. He was fine with it. On the way to Marilyn's hotel, I picked up a couple of steaks. Howard's garden had a little grill. I amazed myself that I was able to cook the steaks without having the fire go out. This was new to me. Marilyn helped me with the vegetables. When I opened a bottle of Howard's wine, I spilled some of it on us, but we got past that and had a leisurely dinner. After we finished, we went outside to watch the moonlight on the water. We were quiet. There was something in the air. Something between us. Anticipation. A suppressed excitement. That feeling you get that makes your legs feel weak and strong at the same time. I knew something was going to happen. So did Marilyn.

Around two o'clock in the morning we went into the bedroom. I pulled off my shirt. Marilyn stripped down to her panties and bra. Then she sat down on the edge of the bed. I looked at her. She was magnificent. I sat down next to her. We started to kiss and caress each other. I undid her bra. Her breasts were beautifully shaped. We began to make love.

Being with Marilyn was satisfying, so satisfying. The experience was more than just being with a new girl. There was something about her, a mixture of power and vulnerability. It made her unique. Even at this stage of her life, there was something indefinable about her, a sensual presence. It made her lovemaking remarkable.

After this, our first time together, Marilyn and I continued to see each other. She made it clear, though, that we couldn't be seen in public. I could understand that. She was on her way up. I was, too, and what I did in private was my business, not the studio's. Then, as now, Hollywood was a hotbed of gossip. I mentioned Hedda Hopper earlier. She helped me, yes, by mentioning me in her column. But if I'd had information about somebody and didn't give it to her, that would have been the end of my progress. That's how those gossip columnists were—Hedda Hopper, Louella Parsons, Walter Winchell, and Sidney Skolsky, that creepy little guy who attached himself to Marilyn like the parasite that he was. So Marilyn and I had to keep a low profile. I'd pick her up after dark and drive her to Howard's with the top up.

Looking back on that time, I know that Marilyn was the first woman I truly felt close to. She was my first adult relationship. It was a beautiful, precious thing. We came to depend on each other in a funny kind of way, like two kids coming to summer camp and trying to figure it out together. Our feelings were genuine. Sadly, they couldn't survive the pressure cooker of Hollywood life. There were too many demands on us. I was making pictures back to back. She was studying and trying to make contacts. We were just too young to embark on a serious relationship. I often wonder what would have happened if I'd met her at the factory where she was working only a few years earlier, if I'd been a shift worker, too. Maybe we would have had a chance. But not two kids hell-bent on stardom. I was preoccupied with Universal, and she was searching for the older man who could both replace her father and shine a spotlight on her. That sure as hell wasn't me. But for the short time that we were together, we had a sweet, intense connection. I'll never forget it.

About four years later, I was at a Hollywood party and all of a sudden I saw Marilyn in the distance. We got closer, and the first thing she said was, "What happened to your green convertible?" I laughed, and as I was laughing I marveled at how she'd evolved, this blond beauty, so glazed and poised. Was this the same girl? Yes and no. There'd been changes—in both of us. And, as I'd discover on the set of *Some Like It Hot*, those changes hadn't brought peace of mind.

7

The idea of working with Marilyn Monroe on *Some Like It Hot* excited me. And made me a little anxious. Would the old feelings resurface? I was married. She was married. Arthur Miller was the playwright famous for *All My Sons, Death of a Salesman*, and *The Crucible*. By this time, their marriage was not a happy

one. Like mine, it was publicized as happy. In actuality it was
something else. Marilyn had thought that by marrying this brainy
guy, she could move into a different arena and turn her back on
Hollywood. For the last two years, she'd tried that. She'd formed
her own production company and made a picture in England
with Laurence Olivier, *The Prince and the Showgirl*. But it didn't
do that well and didn't open any doors. And besides, she owed
Twentieth Century–Fox some pictures. She tried to escape but
couldn't.

I later learned that Marilyn had had a miscarriage in August
1957. I'd heard there were problems because of the abortions
she'd had earlier. That was probably gossip. She'd had a series
of ectopic pregnancies, where the fetus develops in the fallopian
tube instead of in the uterus. She'd had surgery to correct this
but still couldn't have a normal pregnancy. The latest miscarriage was the worst. It caused her to be depressed. She stayed
in her bed, unable to motivate herself to get up and get dressed.
She would lie around without any clothes on and eat all kinds of
fattening foods.

Marilyn was already in the habit of drinking either Bloody
Marys or champagne in the morning. She had terrible insom-
nia. She was taking barbiturates called Amytal and Nembutal.
She was careless. She overdosed twice in early 1958. Her stomach had to be pumped. There was an accident in late March.
She stumbled down a flight of stairs and cut herself on a broken drinking glass. It had contained alcohol. During this time
she was pulling away from Miller. He tried to reach her, but he
couldn't. She withdrew. He stayed in his study, fighting writer's
block.

MGM offered Marilyn a project with Frank Sinatra called
Some Came Running. Twentieth offered her a film of the musical
comedy *Can-Can*. She couldn't make up her mind. But she was
trying to improve it. She was seeing a psychiatrist every morning,
and she was studying with Lee Strasberg every afternoon. When
Billy Wilder heard that she was going to the Actors Studio, he
said, "If Marilyn wants to go to school, she should go to engineer-
ing school and learn to run on time."

Marlon Brando came from the Actors Studio. We were room-mates for four months in a little house on Barham Boulevard. I'd heard about Method acting from him. I respected him. But I wasn't interested in the Method. He was great because he was Marlon, not because of the Method. I thought it was phony. Why complicate the job of acting? Memorize your lines. Learn the part. Find out what the director wants. Then show up on time and act. This idea of trying to remember when your sister stole your peanut butter sandwich so you can give an angry performance is bullshit. If you can't turn it on by yourself, you don't belong in front of a camera.

I heard that Strasberg was exploiting Marilyn. She was desper-ate to get out of the dumb blonde mold. Strasberg played on her desperation, telling her that no one understood how intelligent she was. But he did. Oh, yeah. And it cost her. She became depend-ent on him and his wife, Paula. They were the ones who told her she had to see a psychiatrist—and they supplied the psychiatrist. Miller despised them, but he put up with them. In his own way he was manipulating Marilyn, too. She was constantly being pushed or pulled by somebody. She wasn't strong enough to stand alone. After a childhood without a mother or a father, how could she?

Marilyn was not unintelligent. She was bright, perceptive, and insightful—but only about other people. When it came to her-self, or to issues relating to herself, she didn't have a clue. She needed constant reassurance. She almost didn't sign the Mirisch contract. She was overcome with uncertainty. After she first read Billy's synopsis, she became upset. She'd left Hollywood because she was sick of playing dumb blondes. What was this? The story of a blonde so dumb that she can't tell that these women weren't really women. One day Marilyn threw the papers onto the floor. Miller tried to reason with her. She didn't want to listen. So who did she go to? Mr. Strasberg.

"Lee, I've got a real problem," she said. "I just can't believe in the central situation. I'm supposed to be real cozy with these two newcomers, who are really men in drag. Now how can I pos-sibly feel a thing like that? After all, I know the two are men." Strasberg had to think about that one.

"Well, that shouldn't be too difficult, Marilyn," Lee began.
"You know it's always been difficult for you to have a relationship
with women. They're jealous of you. When you come into a room,
all the men flock around, but women kind of keep their distance.
So you've never been able to make a true woman friend."

"That's almost true."

"A lot of men have wanted to be your friend, but you haven't
had a girl friend. Now here suddenly are two women, and they
want to be your friends! They like you. For the first time in your
life, you have two girl friends."

Marilyn was momentarily soothed. But she was still irresolute.

"Should I do my next picture or stay home and try to have a
baby again?" she wrote to her friend Norman Rosten. "I'd probably make a kooky mother; I'd love my child to death. I want it,
yet I'm scared. Arthur says he wants it, but he's losing his enthu-
siasm. He thinks I should do the picture. After all, I'm a movie
star, right?" In late April she signed the contract with the Mirisch
Company.

On April 25, Billy sent a telegram to New York. "Dear Marilyn:
I am genuinely delighted to have you aboard. Hope to see both
you and Arthur soon in Smogsville, at which time I would also
like to discuss the *Misfits* script. Affectionately, Billy." Miller was
writing a screenplay based on his short story "The Misfits," which
had appeared in *Esquire* a year earlier. The writing was not going
well. Marilyn was trying to be both supportive and unobtrusive,
but Miller's anxiety was starting to tell on the relationship.

Meanwhile, Billy and Izzy were in their office writing *Some
Like It Hot*. They were across the hall from Walter Mirisch, so
they would go to lunch with him. Obviously he was interested in
what they were coming up with. The work wasn't glamorous. Billy
compared himself and Izzy to bank tellers, coming in at nine and
plugging away at the thing all day. But writing is mysterious. How
do you do it, especially with another guy? First of all, they divided
the labor, in part because they were different. Billy was kinetic.
He liked to move around. He didn't like sitting. He was always
pacing back and forth, throwing ideas around the room, some of
which Izzy would catch, some of which floated into the ether. Izzy

was content to sit at the typewriter, like he was driving a car. He'd take everything down, all the crazy thoughts. He liked typing. Billy didn't. He didn't like being stuck behind the typewriter. It made him uncomfortable, and it was boring.

They would work on the overall structure first, then make sure all the funny ideas fit. That's probably how they knew that the musicians needed only one disguise. That was funny enough. But who knows what they really thought, what ideas were flying around that office? I heard that they acted out scenes to make sure they played. Billy would play one character. Izzy would play the other. They would decide every element there, rather than having Izzy go off and dream something up and come back to show it to Billy. No. They agreed where the thing was going, got it down, and then Izzy would go home and type up the draft. The next day Billy would look at it. "Mm hm," he would say. "Okay. Now . . . let's see what we can do to make it better." There'd be a lot of smoking, maybe a cocktail at lunch, but mostly batting ideas back and forth. Once in a while they'd hit a dry patch, and there would be silence for hours. But not often. Once they'd gotten rolling, they had momentum.

One thing I found interesting: they would start a picture with an incomplete script. As they were making the picture, they saw it go in directions they hadn't expected, and they wanted to be able to follow that lead. I know this happened on our picture.

While the script was growing, Billy was thinking about who could play Joe, the other musician. One night he was having dinner with his wife, Audrey, at Dominick's on Beverly Boulevard in West Hollywood. In those days it was a modest little place with red-checkered tablecloths. Billy looked up and saw Jack Lemmon sitting with his girlfriend, Felicia Farr. Billy waved across the room to Jack, who immediately came to his table.

"Do me a favor," said Billy. "Sit down for a minute. I have an idea for a picture I would like you to play in."

"We've just ordered," said Jack. "Could I see you in a few minutes?"

"We'll stop by your table on our way out," said Billy.

Jack sat down and waited. You can imagine that he was a little anxious. Finally Billy and Audrey came over.

"Listen to this idea," said Billy.

"Sit down," said Jack. "Please. I want to hear all about it."

"I haven't got time to tell you everything now," said Billy, "but I'll give you a rough idea. It's about two men on the lam from gangsters, running for their lives. They dress up in girls' clothes and join an all-girl orchestra."

"They do. Hm."

"Which means that you'll play three quarters of the film in drag. At least."

"Uh huh." Jack was looking Billy in the eye. But he was thinking, Oh, Jesus Christ. We're in drag and everything. But wait a minute. Billy Wilder is doing it. It's not going to be in bad taste.

"Do you want to do it?" asked Billy.

"I'll do it if I'm free to do it," said Jack. "And if I'm not free, I'll get free."

"Terrific," said Billy. "I'll send you some pages."

I'd known Jack for some time. He was a good friend of an artist that I knew, Joseph Cornell. Jack was at Columbia Pictures. We'd become friends because we were both young guys with contracts, making a proper living as actors. I'd see him at parties. Then Jack won the Oscar for *Mister Roberts* and moved to a different echelon. Even though Danny Kaye kept after Billy to be in this film, Billy kept saying no. He had me, and he knew that he had to find just the right guy to play my friend. Maybe Danny would have overwhelmed me. Maybe I would have made him look old. For whatever reason, Billy said no to Danny. "I want this kid Lemmon from Columbia," he decided all of a sudden. Jack said later that he would have run like a jackrabbit if any other director had asked him to play a transvestite. "Everybody in town thought that Wilder had lost his marbles," Jack told me. "How can you put two stars in drag for that much of a movie? That's a five-minute sketch, not a movie." But Billy had a unique track record. "I admired what he had done in the past," said Jack. "Immensely."

Jack didn't hear from Billy for months after their conversation at Dominick's. Then a messenger brought a package to Jack's home in Bel Air. It contained sixty pages of script. Jack lay down on his couch to read it. "They were the greatest sixty pages I ever read," he told me. "I laughed so hard that I fell off the couch! Literally!" He jumped in his car and drove to Goldwyn. He burst into Billy's office, holding the script.

"Billy! Where's the rest of this?"

"You won't get it until we're shooting," Billy told him.

And that's when Jack learned that Billy started shooting with an unfinished script.

About the same time I was at Harold Mirisch's house for another movie party. Up walked Billy.

"I'm not going to use Sinatra," he said to me. "He's going to be too much trouble."

"What kind of trouble?"

"He'll have to dress up as a woman every day, and I just can't see Frank doing that."

At this point I was wondering if I could do it. But I nodded and listened. Billy looked around the room and continued.

"I'm going to use Jack Lemmon instead."

What Billy did next was switch our roles. Instead of playing Jerry, the crazy bass player, I would play Joe, the randy sax player. Jack would play Jerry. Marilyn would play Stella, now renamed Sugar. With this lineup, the whole project came to life. The balance of the story changed. That combination was happy; that chemistry was vibrant. That's how pictures are made.

Billy's casting coup didn't end with the principals. He also cast the supporting parts: the girls, the gangsters, and Osgood the eccentric millionaire. Billy Wilder was a great baseball fan. He always attended the season opener. This was a big one. The Dodgers were starting their first season as a Los Angeles team. The opening ceremonies on April 18 included a parade and a celebrity luncheon to benefit the Los Angeles Orphanage Guild. The master of ceremonies at the Biltmore Bowl was Joe E. Brown. This guy was a booster. In those days baseball games were played at the Coliseum. Joe E. was campaigning to have a stadium built above Sunset. (He would eventually dedicate Dodger Stadium.) Billy took a look at Joe E. and recognized him from

1930s Warner Bros. comedies. "This is the guy," Billy said out loud. "Osgood. The crazy guy. Joe E. Brown. He's old enough and he looks loony enough."

Billy told me that he was going to have George Raft play the gangster Spats Columbo and Edward G. Robinson play the big boss Little Bonaparte. They'd made a Warner Bros. picture in 1941 called *Manpower*, directed by Raoul Walsh. Billy liked the combination, so he wanted to put them together again. But there was a problem he'd forgotten. Or maybe he didn't know about it.

While Raft and Robinson were making *Manpower*, they both got interested in the leading lady, Marlene Dietrich. They became rivals. There was tension on the set. One day it blew up, and they came to blows. Unfortunately, it was the same day that the publicist had a *Life* magazine photographer there. He caught the fistfight. *Life* magazine ran the picture. There wasn't a goddamned thing that Warners could do about it. If it had been the unit stills photographer, Warners could have destroyed the film and paid those old bitches Hedda Hopper and Louella Parsons to write about how much Raft and Robinson respected each other. But there was no way that Warners could bribe *Life*. The picture ran. And the story. Robinson vowed never to work with Raft again.

Billy also had a history with Raft. He'd offered him *Double Indemnity*. Raft turned him down. Imagine. Of course, Raft had turned down *High Sierra*, *The Maltese Falcon*, and *Casablanca*, too. Humphrey Bogart accepted those roles and became a star. When Raft turned down *Double Indemnity*, Billy told some columnist that he was sure that it was going to be a great picture—because Raft had turned it down.

In 1958 Billy either didn't know about Robinson's attitude toward Raft or thought he'd get over it. As the budget was being drawn up, Robinson was still part of the package. In Billy's mind, *Some Like It Hot* was cast.

Billy and Izzy completed their first draft (except for the ending, of course) on May 2, so Walter Mirisch submitted the budget to United Artists. It came to $2,373,490. Marilyn Monroe would get $200,000. I would get $100,000 against 5 percent of the gross over $2 million. Jack Lemmon would get the same. Izzy Diamond would get $60,000. Because Billy was producing, directing, and cowriting, he would get $200,000 plus 17.5 percent of the gross above double the negative cost. But if the picture grossed $1 million (or more) after it broke even, Billy would get 20 percent. You can see why talent wanted to work with UA. Of course, Arthur Krim was a touch nervous, what with the huge salaries and Marilyn's reputation for slowing things down. But there was nothing much to worry about. In the third week of July, we reported to the studio for tests. You can't start a picture without tests—especially if you're going to be in drag.

Part III

The Preproduction

8

I started to get excited about *Some Like It Hot* in June. So did Hollywood. When people heard that Marilyn Monroe was returning, it was like the circus was coming to town. Everyone in the press started jockeying for position, fighting for assignments. Hedda Hopper got there first. She had to fly to New York to scoop her rival Louella, but she did it. This was the first coverage of Marilyn's involvement in the project. Marilyn and Arthur Miller had an apartment at 444 East Fifty-seventh Street. That's where Hedda interviewed them. Arthur started talking first, then excused himself to get back to his typewriter. "I'm working on a novel," he explained. "*The Misfits*. I'm doing a screenplay of it, too. And I'm writing a new play. Don't ask me when any of them will be finished. I don't know. I'm not a fast writer."

Hedda wanted to know how Marilyn felt about working in a comedy. Would she be able to jump from drama to comedy and back again? And how about the atmosphere on the set? Would she be nervous? "I'm not a quick study," Marilyn began. "I'm not experienced enough as an actress to chat with friends and workers on the set and then go straight into a difficult dramatic scene. Some actors can chat and laugh and then go straight into a serious mood before the camera. I can't. I like to go directly from my dressing room to the scene. After that, I go back to my dressing room and concentrate on the next one. I like to keep my mind in one channel. All I can think of is my performance. I like to make it as good as I know how."

We were originally scheduled to start makeup and wardrobe tests in early July, but there was an accident. Samuel Goldwyn, besides renting space to the Mirisches and Billy, was making a

48

picture in his own studio. It was a big one. *Porgy and Bess*, with Sidney Poitier, Sammy Davis Jr., and Dorothy Dandridge. Rouben Mamoulian had directed both the original DuBose Heyward play and George Gershwin's *Porgy and Bess* on Broadway. He was going to direct the film. Goldwyn had a sprawling set built on Stage 8: Catfish Row. It was the largest set yet built in Hollywood, an amazing set, full of texture and detail. I enjoyed walking on new sets, seeing what the technicians had come up with. I loved studio work. The magic of moviemaking, how those worlds were created.

On July 2, just before *Porgy and Bess* was to start shooting, somebody left a cigarette burning on the set. Fire broke out. Stage 8, the second largest soundstage in Hollywood, was destroyed, and with it, thirty years of props and costumes, including Irene Sharaff's costumes for the film. The Goldwyn studio was in a state of chaos.

Marilyn flew into Los Angeles on Tuesday, July 8. The talk around town was that she was washed up. The exhibitors and fan magazine polls in late 1957 had showed Liz Taylor, Debbie Reynolds, and Natalie Wood as top box-office draws. Marilyn hadn't even placed. As I later found out, there's nothing Hollywood enjoys more than a falling star. It likes to put stars on a pedestal. It *loves* to pull them down. This was evident from the press Marilyn got while we were making *Some Like It Hot*. Every article acknowledged her star status, and every article made cracks.

"Marilyn Monroe gloriously preserved her reputation for late arrivals yesterday," wrote Jack Smith in the *Los Angeles Times*. "She did the seemingly impossible by arriving half an hour late aboard a Trans World Airlines plane that was on time." I'm sure Marilyn could sense the hostility in the journalists and photographers waiting outside her plane at seven in the morning. They made no secret of it. "She's taking longer than that duck-billed platypus," said one reporter loudly, referring to the creature that had recently been flown to the Bronx Zoo.

When Marilyn finally emerged from the plane, sounds of adulation rose from the waiting crowd. "Monroe is the only star that the fans will get up this early to come and see," observed an airport guard who was busy holding them back. A cyclone fence stretched with the pressure of another group, airline mechanics who made approving noises at the sight of Marilyn. "Breathing deeply and licking her lips, Miss Monroe fluttered thick black eyelashes at a row of grease monkeys," wrote Smith. "Then, white hair aswirl in the propwash of another plane; white silk shirt open at the powdered white throat; white, tight silk skirt, white shoes, white gloves, Marilyn Monroe blinked big, sleepy eyes at the world. She brushed a hank of white hair from her forehead and began descending—slowly and wickedly—down the steps."

Reporters commented on Marilyn's new hair color. It was no longer gold, but platinum. "It's White Blonde," she explained. "That's what I call it. I had it done about a week ago for my new picture." Reporters shouted questions about *Some Like It Hot*. What was it about? What did she play? "I haven't read the script yet," she answered. "But I trust Billy Wilder completely." Smith also commented on Marilyn's figure. "Miss Monroe took another step down the ladder and the white skirt stretched tight as a drumhead over her ample hips." Yes, said Marilyn, she may have put on just a little weight. "It's still in the right places, isn't it?" she asked. She did not explain that moodiness caused her to lie in bed all day, imbibing champagne and ingesting chocolate. "I'll be in good shape in two weeks. I intend to do lots of walking and exercising." She said that Arthur Miller had stayed behind to work on his play. Was he writing a part for her in it? "Who knows?" she answered.

A limousine took Marilyn to the Bel Air Hotel, where she would live while we were making *Some Like It Hot*. I was preparing for my first public appearance in connection with the movie. A "press reception" (not to be confused with a press conference) was scheduled for five thirty that afternoon. Billy had been working with the public relations firm of Rogers and Cowan to make sure that the picture would be presented properly, or, as now they say about a product, "positioned." There had never been a big-budget comedy with female impersonators before, so it had to be handled just right. A press reception was the first step. Jack Lemmon wouldn't be there. He was in Chester, Connecticut, making a movie with Doris Day.

Billy, George, and I walked into the Rodeo Room of the Beverly Hills Hotel at five forty-five. We could hear the snarls.

"Curtis looks like he's gonna play a trombone player in *The Music Man*," somebody whispered.

"I've been here since five. When is Monroe going to show up?"

"She's always very late," said someone else. "It's because she's afraid. She has to convince herself to do this."

"I'll bet you even money she doesn't walk through that door before seven fifteen," said a woman editor.

"You're on," said a photographer as he dug into his wallet.

Billy, George, and I took our places behind a table. "I've been working on pictures for thirty years now," Billy began. "There's nothing tougher or more challenging than farce. It's like juggling eleven meringue pies at once. Let one drop and you're dead. This whole picture is farce, in the manner of the Twenties. Besides Tony and Jack and Marilyn, I am getting together as many great gangsters of the period as I can—Pat O'Brien, George, and, for a one-scene finish, Eddie Robinson." A reporter asked Billy why he was using Marilyn in a period film; she was a modern personality. Billy answered that Marilyn could play any era. "It's that little-girl quality she has. She's not resented by men's wives the way her imitators are." There were chuckles and murmurs of Jayne Mansfield and Diana Dors.

At six, there was a stir from the hallway. Then a rumble. Footsteps. Voices. Urgency. Marilyn was coming. I'd been mobbed by fans. I'd had my clothes torn. You expected that. But to see members of the press go wild was something else again. You could tell how agitated they were by how hard they tried to conceal it. And by the tone of their articles. "Marilyn Monroe is back, looking like a glorious caricature of herself," wrote Philip K. Scheuer in the *Times*. "In the grandest movie-queen tradition she swept into the Rodeo Room, swinging that celebrated torso, now more legendary than factual." Gene Sherman was equally tart. He wrote:

She wore long white gloves, a dress she later told someone was a braless, girdleless sheath, no stockings, and
black spike shoes. She paused and poked at her platinum
locks as she wobbled inside. (The word is not meant to be
uncomplimentary—she just walks funny.) The photographers clustered around her immediately and thereafter
moved with her as an entity. She opened her eyes wide
and worked her mouth strangely in unison with the flash
guns. She was piloted around the room by a small cordon
of young men, greeting people she recognized and smiling
at others. When she wasn't smiling she was working her
mouth and batting her eyes. Occasionally she lifted one
leg slightly and rubbed its calf against the other.

With all that was going on that day, Marilyn barely said hello to
me. I was a little disappointed. I'd hoped for a few words at least.
But the reception was a success. We'd alerted the world. Now all
we had to do was make the picture.

9

Our preproduction work began on July 21, after Jack returned
from Connecticut and finished his film with Doris Day at
Columbia. They played well together. He hoped to work with
her again, but it never happened. That's how it is when you're an
actor; most of the time it's not up to you. For example, when Jack
arrived, we had to pick up our costumes. We'd already had our fit-
tings: Jack's in Connecticut, and mine at Goldwyn. But when it was
time for our wardrobe, they sent us to Western Costume, which
was the place that rented second-hand costumes to studios. And
we were supposed to be stars! But we took ourselves over there,
ready to put up with some odd looks. We weren't going there for
men's costumes, but for women's.

In 1958 I was the happiest of fellows. I was a movie star with a string of hits. What more could anyone want? Well, there was something.

I wanted the opportunity to make a superior motion picture. It came to me in the form of an invitation from Billy Wilder. He asked me to play in *Some Like It Hot* and then hired the gifted Jack Lemmon.

Although Some *Like It Hot* was an independent film made at the end of the big-studio era, the Mirisch Company had us working on one of the grand old lots, the Samuel Goldwyn studio.

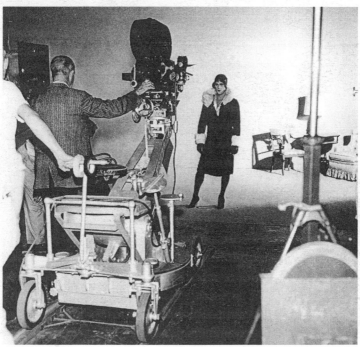

I was getting into character as Josephine as early as the makeup and costume tests. But Billy and I decided that my drag persona should be genteel and reserved. Oh, well.

Jack Lemmon and I posed for lots of photos in character as Josephine and Daphne.

This photo was taken in the commissary at the Samuel Goldwyn studio, where I ate lunch. I'm introducing myself to the manager on my first day of work. I usually had breakfast with Jack at the Formosa Café.

Some Like It Hot was a period picture, but they didn't give us dresses from the twenties. They gave us dresses that looked like they'd been made in the forties for movies that took place in the twenties. I don't know who wore them. Maybe Eve Arden or Loretta Young. Who knows? But they didn't do a thing for me. They didn't fit right. They puckered up. I knew this. My father was a tailor. I didn't like the idea that they were passing this shit off as wardrobe on a $2 million picture. I drove back to the studio and marched into Billy's office. "Uh, Billy," I said. "Who's designing Marilyn's gowns?

"Orry-Kelly."

"He's really good. Why can't he design the dresses for me and Jack? I don't want these hand-me-downs. Can't you have Orry-Kelly make our dresses?"

"All right," said Billy. "We'll have him make yours, too."

I felt that Billy handled it well. I'm not sure what Orry-Kelly thought when he got the news.

While the gowns were being made, Jack and I had special training. And I do mean special. Billy remembered a man from his wild young days in Europe. The man's name was Barbette. Once I heard the name, I had a clue. Barbette was a famous female impersonator. He was originally from Texas but had made a name for himself on the Continent. Billy's plan was to have Barbette instruct Jack and me in the fine art—or was it science—of transvestism. We dutifully reported for lessons with Barbette on a stage at Goldwyn. Billy told Barbette that he shouldn't make us too convincing. The guys in the story are doing drag out of necessity, not preference. Billy wanted us to look like we were trying hard but not quite getting it, at least from our point of view. Then the audience could sympathize with us. And laugh at us. If we took to it too quickly, we'd be suspect, not funny.

Barbette showed us things we'd never heard of. Or thought of. And we were trained actors. I mean, in the navy they taught us to keep our butts tight, but I never did hear of sitting with the palms of your hands down so that you don't flex your biceps. And then there was this business of walking with your legs slightly crossed in front. "Always cross one foot in front of the other," said

Barbette. "That makes your hips do something special." No kidding. They might as well have had neon signs on them, saying "Look here!"

"When you walk forward," Barbette persisted, "cross one foot over the other. You'll walk like a lady. You'll swivel your hips. It's feminine."

I managed it because it was kind of like dancing, an athletic discipline. And there was nothing athletic I couldn't do. But Jack wasn't getting it. In fact, he was resisting. "I don't want to do that," he said. "Nobody really does that. Man *or* woman. And besides, Jerry and Joe should each get into this drag thing differently. You're trying to make us do it exactly the same, like we're in formation." Jack was not going along with the program. Barbette was not pleased.

One afternoon, Jack and I reported for our lessons as usual. Barbette was nowhere in sight. We waited. Jack's expression lightened a bit. Then he suggested we go to Billy's office. When we got there, Billy had a wry look on his face.

"Where's Barbette?" I asked.

"I booked him passage on the *Ile de France*."

"What?"

"He came to me and said, 'Tony is wonderful, Billy. He'll be perfect. But this Lemmon! He is totally *impossible*. He refuses to do what I tell him. I wash my hands of it.' And he left."

Jack maintained that he was right. "Billy," he said, "you don't want both of us doing the same shtick. Tony's character should be like Tony. Skillful. Successful at the imitation. I'm clumsy. The shoes are killing me. My ankles are turning. I'm scared shitless. But Tony can carry it off. He puts his head up in the air and purses his lips."

By this time, our characters had female names. My Joe was to become Josephine. Jerry was to become Geraldine, except that in a moment of brilliantly insightful writing, Billy and Izzy had Jerry taken over by the character he's playing. Instead of mechanically saying his name is Geraldine, the obvious feminization of his own name, Jerry blurts out: "I'm Daphne!" He becomes not merely a man playing a woman, but a willful persona. Pretty amazing for 1958.

The whole thing was so amazing that it scared me. Part of it was the process. We had to have our legs and chests shaved and our eyebrows plucked a bit. We had to be padded, of course, and some things had to be hidden. The makeup artists were two consummate pros, Emile LaVigne and Harry Ray. They'd done every picture from *The Wizard of Oz* to *Friendly Persuasion*. Wonderful, patient guys. They took us through a series of tests: wigs, eyelashes, lipsticks, foundations. When they put the ensemble together for the first time, I was surprised how I felt. Uncomfortable. Awkward. Self-conscious. But Jack was, all of a sudden, enjoying himself, laughing and carrying on. I froze when Billy came into the makeup department.

"What's the matter, Tony?"

"I'm not going out there."

"Come on, come on."

But I was petrified. Maybe it said something about the years I'd put up with guys coming on to me and saying things about me. Or maybe it was some kind of strange thing I felt about my mother. I don't know. I felt like my manhood was being threatened at a very deep level. It was difficult. But I'm proud of the way I finally got past it. I took some deep breaths and reminded myself of the challenges I'd met on the streets of New York and in the navy and in the picture business. I'd gotten through those. By comparison this was nothing. I grabbed a purse and took the first step outside.

There were about fifty people standing in the studio street, waiting to see what I looked like as Josephine. Oh, no. I blushed under the makeup and let the actor in me take over. I launched into a little routine. I was coy. I was reluctant. I put my hand over my face, using the postures Barbette had shown me.

When Jack came out, he did it in a big way. He was in character as Daphne. He flew out, twirling and pirouetting. He danced. He shrieked. He pranced. I just stared. How the fuck could he do that? I was envious, but it was the first and last time. I loved the guy.

Back in the makeup department the next day, something came over me. I turned to Jack and said, "Listen, Jack. I'm sorry, but you don't make a good-looking woman." I didn't want to hurt his feelings but I felt that he should know. He was ugly as a woman. I was more attractive, but that's genetics, I guess. Then I had an idea.

"We may look good on the set. And we may not. But how do we look in real life?"

"You mean out in the world? Not in front of a camera? I don't know."

"Why don't we test it?" I asked.

"Test it? Where?"

"Let's go to the ladies' room."

"I don't think I want to do that."

"Come on," I said, getting up and pulling him by the arm. "Let's just try it out."

We walked out of the makeup department and down the studio street. Gaining momentum, we marched past the commissary, into the ladies' room, and up to the mirrors. There were a couple of women there, adjusting their makeup. I took out my lipstick. Women were walking in and out. They'd come out of the stalls, walk up behind us, wash their hands, and then start freshening their makeup in the mirror next to us. It was strange. No one gave me or Jack a second look. After a bit, we nodded to each other and left the ladies' room.

"We made it," said Jack.

"No," I said, shaking my head. "It isn't that. It's that we're so ugly. They don't even *see* us."

"No!"

We went back to Emile and Harry. "Guys," I said, "you gotta make us a little better looking. Figure something out."

So they tried putting on more mascara and darker eye shadow. Larger falsies. Three-inch heels instead of two-inch. Tighter waistlines. We went back to the ladies' room. Right in the doorway, a girl stopped and looked at me.

"Hi, Tony!" she said cheerfully.

"Let's go," I said to Jack.

So much for the "better-looking" makeup. Billy didn't agree. He saw us and was thrilled. He knew we'd gotten it. "That's it," he exclaimed. "Keep it! Lock it! Boom!"

So we did. I tried to think of my Josephine as a combination of that gorgeous silent-movie actress Dolores Costello, the elegant Grace Kelly, and, last but not least, my mother. A funny thing happened when Jack's mother came to see him and he was dressed as Daphne. They took a picture together. When he saw the picture he thought that the two of them looked like sisters. It was strange. And at the same time reassuring. You never wander too far from your roots.

10

It all comes down to your roots. Jack had a fairly happy childhood. He had respect and encouragement. I didn't. I had to fight for everything I wanted, whether at home or on the street. My roots were tangled and twisted. I had to go far and struggle hard to get away from that tangle. But at least I had roots. What about Marilyn? I don't want to sound like an armchair psychologist, but I think her problems came from the fact that she had no roots. The articles about her at the time talked about her "homecoming." Homecoming? To what home? She had no home. She never felt like she belonged anywhere. She was always trying to survive in somebody else's space. She had none of her own.

She was living with Arthur Miller in an apartment near Sutton Place in New York, but she felt like she was leasing a tiny corner of his world. None of it belonged to her, even though she was famous and rich. She felt powerless, at the mercy of other people. That's why she had to retreat every once in a while, just to preserve a sense of herself. That's why she would hide out in her dressing room. She was trying to put down roots somewhere, anywhere, so she'd have some feeling of security, however temporary it might be. Anyway, this so-called homecoming meant that she was back in Los Angeles, but nowhere she'd lived before. While she worked on *Some Like It Hot*, she would be staying in a suite at the Bel Air Hotel.

The suite was modern and airy, but not very homey. It cost $65 a day. It had a living room, a den, a full kitchen, a small patio, and a large bedroom. There was a piano in the living room because she had to learn songs for the picture. She bought a parakeet not long after she arrived because she was lonesome for the dog she had in New York. His name was Hugo. He was a huge beagle. I visited Marilyn at her hotel room with Billy one day. I could see how she might be lonesome. She had to sneak in and out through a back entrance. She had few visitors. No calls were put through except from Billy or Arthur Miller. It was a luxurious prison.

Marilyn didn't have female friends, but she always had a woman around her. When she came out to California this time, the woman was May Reis. She was a nice lady in her fifties. She'd been Marilyn's secretary for three years. Before that she'd worked for Elia Kazan and Arthur Miller. Marilyn needed older people around her to stabilize her, I guess, but then, every so often, she'd rebel against them. I can understand it. You need them, and then you don't need them. As I said, it's all about your roots—or lack of them. I'd been seeing a psychiatrist for two years, trying to figure it out. It was expensive and it was difficult.

My home life at this point was strained. It had been for some time. Being married is not easy. Of course being single isn't easy, either. You don't have a lot of choices in life, do you? I don't like to disappoint people. From my earliest consciousness, I always felt that more than anything else, I wanted people to like me. That was the most important thing. I tried to say things that would make them like me. But almost anything you say can be used as a weapon against you. In Hollywood everybody is trying to make the next deal. If you help them, they act like they like you. If you're not part of that equation, they don't know your name. It's a very stressful way to live. It breeds insecurity. And if you're not sure of yourself, of who you are, it's dangerous. Trying to be liked and at the same time trying to make your way in a competitive environment—the real danger is to your family life.

I had no preparation for getting married and being a father. How could I? My parents acted like every day was a punishment for marrying. They had a miserable life. They were always blaming each other for every damned thing. No sense of responsibility. Just blame somebody else for what you don't like. At one point they were saying that all their problems came from being in the United States. As if they would have prospered in Hungary. The foolishness. The self-deception. The pettiness. It was awful. No wonder I spent so much time on the street, getting into trouble. It was all I could do to get out of there with my mind intact. You hear about role models. I had none. I never saw a happy couple. How could I expect to have a happy life with Janet Leigh?

She was a sweet woman. She was educated. She was cultured. She cared about people. But we were young, and as I say, we were ambitious. You can't go so far so fast without being ambitious. She'd been in Hollywood several years longer than I had, and she'd risen quickly. Being a movie star means that you carry a picture. The audience is there to see you, not the supporting cast or the extras. It's a responsibility, believe me. When Janet married me in 1951, I had just begun carrying my own pictures. She, on the other hand, had been around since 1947, was in demand as a leading lady, but was not quite a star. I didn't see it that way. To me she was an MGM star. And that was the best there was. MGM was the Tiffany of the studios. So I was in awe of Janet, even though I was catching up fast. I thought of myself as an outsider, kind of rough around the edges, and a long way from stardom. Our marriage changed that. The explosion of publicity pushed both of us much farther than we would have gone in the same amount of time if we hadn't gotten married.

We appeared together in a Paramount film called *Houdini*. It was a big hit and it showed Universal how valuable I was. At the same time, Janet got better offers, like *My Sister Eileen*. She even sang in it. But Hollywood doesn't reward you for being versatile. Hollywood rewards you for doing something that makes money over and over again. And you don't want to object to it. I got lots of offers to play a young, good-looking guy with a New York accent, which was exactly what I was trying to escape. Janet told me that I should accept these offers. So did Lew Wasserman. A lot of times when I did accept them, it was because I didn't want to make anyone mad. And Janet would get mad at me if I didn't go along with the program. Well, not mad, exactly. She'd act kind of cold and distant. I wanted desperately to be liked, so I'd give in. But in going against what I wanted, I was setting myself up for bad things.

Janet insisted that we go to a lot of parties. I knew they were important. But so many? She'd insist we go to a party when I'd been working my ass off on a physically demanding film all day. Try going through umpteen emotions and fist fights for twelve hours without getting tired. I would come home exhausted. And she'd be ready to go to a party. Even if I couldn't rest right away, I at least wanted to be alone with her. But no. We had to go to the Feldmans or the Goetzes or some other A-list party. I know it was important, but was every one as important as every other one? And did they have to go so late and serve so much booze when I had to be in front of a camera the next morning?

All of this frantic activity was driving a wedge between me and Janet. Sure, I was with her at the party, but I wasn't really *with* her. We were in the same room, but talking to different people. I'd be in a corner with Gene Kelly. She'd be at the bar drinking with Debbie Reynolds. We might as well have gone there separately. Sometimes I would just sit by myself, nursing a drink, and watch the people. Cary Grant. Clark Gable. Errol Flynn. I would hear them talk from across the room, then maybe say hello. I was careful not to bother a big star. I didn't want to be told to get away and not bother him. But that didn't happen. They were gentlemen. And what I learned, after I heard them talking about the problems that they had with their agents or contracts or getting the right picture was that they were mortal. We all were. Regardless of what the publicity departments wrote about us, or how they photographed us, we were all mortal. And we knew it. So I lost my fantasies about people in the movies, and I lost my fantasy about being married to a movie star.

The way things were going with Janet, I had very little personal life. Not that Hollywood allowed stars to have personal lives, but I wanted something for myself. And I felt like she was too busy and too organized to be spontaneous about something as unplanned as lovemaking. That was the reason we'd gotten married. We couldn't keep our hands off each other. We were always so hot. We couldn't be apart. It was wonderful to feel like that, even if it didn't have much to do with the reality of carving out a career in a hostile environment. But love isn't supposed to have much to do with reality. By 1958 the reality was that we had one child and were expecting another, but we were living separate lives. We were rarely intimate. I still had needs. I started going outside my home to satisfy them.

Nicky Blair, who had a restaurant, gave me the address of a girl who lived up in the hills. I would drive up there, park my car carefully so that it wouldn't roll down the hill, and then meet this girl. Her little house was in L.A., but high enough in the hills so that it felt like I was away from everything. I'd spend a few hours up there with her. It was different. It was like climbing to heaven. It wasn't just the idea of going there for a sexual act. It was more like I was the character I'd played in *The Prince Who Was a Thief* or *Son of Ali Baba*. It was exotic and transporting, and it satisfied my needs for a time. Ultimately, though, I felt demeaned. I developed feelings of shame.

Obviously I couldn't discuss this with Janet. I couldn't confront her about our alienation. My frustrations weren't her fault, but at the time I thought they were. I didn't know what she was thinking. I thought that maybe she envied my progress. I was gaining ground with pictures like *Kings Go Forth*. *Sweet Smell of Success* hadn't been a hit. It was too caustic for the average moviegoer, I guess. But I got sensational reviews. Of course Janet was doing well, too, so there was no reason to be competitive, but I felt that she was. I noticed that when I'd get home, there'd be something in the air. She'd be irritable for no reason. It put me on edge. There'd be this awkward silence. I couldn't stand it. Then, just as I was getting ready to escape, I'd hear the sound of ice cubes dropping into a cocktail glass. Janet would call to me. She'd offer me a drink. I didn't want to displease her, so I accepted. The drinks smoothed things over—for a while. Then we'd have dinner. But when we started to talk about some picture that I didn't want to do, the alcohol would kick in. We'd argue. So I'd end up storming out anyway. I'd drive to Frank Sinatra's or some restaurant bar. There'd be an attractive woman sitting by herself, which might mean that she was a B-girl or even a hooker. I didn't care. I would go with her, as long as she was nice to me. Then I'd come home feeling guilty. And the cycle would start again. No wonder I spent $30,000 on a shrink in four years' time.

There was one party that Janet and I couldn't get out of, even if the idea of going to it made me nervous. It was about a week before we were scheduled to start shooting *Some Like It Hot*. Arthur Miller had flown in to be with Marilyn, so Harold Mirisch thought it would be a nice idea to throw a dinner party so everybody could get acquainted. Janet and I went. Walter Mirisch and his wife, Pat, were there, too, along with Izzy and Barbara Diamond, Billy and Audrey, and a few others. Cocktails were at seven, dinner at eight. We didn't sit down until after nine. Marilyn and Arthur hadn't shown up yet. We ate, had after-dinner drinks, shot the breeze, and waited.

Finally, at twenty past eleven, we heard the doorbell way off in the distance. Sure enough, it was Marilyn and Arthur. Oh, they were so sorry to be late. Blah-blah-blah. Everybody made the best of it. And then Arthur walked up behind Billy and Izzy. He put one arm on each guy's shoulder and started to talk to them about the script. "Now," he said, "the difference between comedy and tragedy is . . . " I tell you, there were some perplexed looks in that room. Billy and Izzy just stood there with faces of stone, listening to this bullshit. Finally Billy rolled his eyes and shifted his weight. Arthur backed off. I could see Marilyn. She was standing off to the side, watching. She looked uneasy. She knew that her husband had made a fool of himself and had insulted Billy's intelligence. It was not a happy scene. It was not a happy way to start a picture.

11

I could tell that we were getting close to starting *Some Like It Hot* when our dressing rooms were rolled onto the first floor of the actor's wing at the Goldwyn studio. First there was Billy's. It had a sign on it: "Gift of Rouben Mamoulian." He was directing *Porgy and Bess* on the next stage. I'd seen a lot of his pictures when I was a kid: *The Mark of Zorro, Blood and Sand, Golden Boy*. That one helped me when I played the lead in the Workshop after the war. Mamoulian was one of the greats, but there had to be a sign on Billy's dressing room to let everyone know that Mamoulian had paid for it. In Hollywood, no one gives you credit unless you demand it. He'd been there thirty years. He knew. Or thought he did. On July 23, Sam Goldwyn fired him from *Porgy and Bess*. Mamoulian was gone, but Billy kept his sign. And when Goldwyn prohibited smoking on the entire lot, Billy put up a sign on our stage: "Come on the Billy Wilder set and smoke your little hearts out." Billy loved his cigarettes. I don't think he loved Sam Goldwyn. The old man was always raising the rent.

The next dressing room on the stage was Jack Lemmon's. Then there was Marilyn's, and then mine. I reported to it for a fitting session with George Orry-Kelly. He was another great talent. He'd designed costumes for all the classic Warner Bros. pictures. Bette Davis owed a lot to him. I found out that he was a good friend of Cary Grant's since the early thirties in New York, when they were roommates. I idolized Cary Grant, plain and simple. Orry-Kelly was constantly on the phone, talking to some woman. I assumed he was gay, so that didn't figure. I later learned that he was talking to Gracie Allen. They were thick as thieves. Even though she'd retired, she wanted to hear all the gossip.

When Orry-Kelly started my fitting, he noticed how fit I was. I was worried that he might think I was a dum-dum who did nothing but lift weights, so I made conversation about my father. I said he was a tailor. Orry-Kelly was interested in that. He cut quite a figure himself. He wore a spotless pin-striped suit, a dress shirt, and a Sulka tie. In his breast pocket he carried a tape measure like my father had—yellow and white, rolled up with a metal fixture at the end. Orry-Kelly made a production of this thing. He took it out of his pocket and then he whipped out the tape in this very grand gesture. It flew out with a whooshing noise. Then he measured me: 16, 34, 43, 18, 19, 18. He had a short man with him. This guy's job was to write down those measurements. Everything's delegated in Hollywood.

Then Orry-Kelly went to Marilyn's trailer. She was waiting. I heard she was reading books in there, odd things like Walt Whitman and Rainer Maria Rilke. When Orry-Kelly went in, she stood up. She was wearing a white blouse, panties, and three-inch heels. Orry-Kelly said hello, and then he took measurements here and there: 37, 24. When he had his tape measure across her hips, he kind of chuckled. "Tony has a better-looking ass than you do."

Marilyn turned around, opened her blouse, and said, "He doesn't have tits like these." Of course it was true. Her breasts were so beautifully arranged. She had the best figure I ever saw in a girl.

She kind of wore out her welcome with Orry-Kelly. After he'd gotten the gowns made, not only for Marilyn, but also for me and Jack, they were rolled to the stage on racks so that we could shoot wardrobe tests. Well, Marilyn was walking by the racks and she got curious. A little while later, Jack came to my dressing room. He looked upset.

"Tony," he said. "You're not gonna believe this."

"What?

"Marilyn took my dress."

"Whaddya mean she took your dress?"

"She stole it. The black one Orry-Kelly made for me. She saw it on the rack and said to the wardrobe mistress, 'Ooh, this looks nice. Let me try it on, huh?' And she decided she had to have it. Orry-Kelly came screaming to me. 'She took your dress! The bitch has pinched your dress!' And they're going to let her get away with it!"

This wasn't the only problem Marilyn caused during preproduction. She argued about makeup and hair. Instead of being dreamy and sexy, she was querulous and demanding. One day I reported to the studio at one thirty to shoot tests with her and Billy. At five thirty she hadn't yet arrived. She hadn't even called. Billy walked out and drove home. At six Marilyn sauntered in. She seemed oblivious to how late she was. I was still there, so the tests were made, even though Billy was no longer present. Since the tests were shot after hours, the Mirisch Company had to pay the crew "golden time," twice the normal rate. That didn't go over so well.

That same week, Marilyn had to record her songs. (You probably know that musical numbers are always shot in lip sync to the playback of the song recorded earlier in a studio.) Her recording session was scheduled for two in the afternoon. The assistant director wasn't taking any chances. He called her at six thirty in the morning. She still arrived fifteen minutes late. No wonder, with the entourage she dragged behind her. There was May Reis. There was Paula Strasberg. And even though no film or photographs were being taken, she brought Jack Cole, her dance director, and Sydney Guilaroff, her hair "designer." She brought everybody but the parakeet.

If these people were there to provide moral support, they did. The session went so well that Marilyn finished an hour early. Amazing. But wait. Two days later, she decided that she wasn't pleased with the results. She wanted to record the three songs again. Back she came. What was more amazing was that she was on time and didn't charge extra for the hours she spent rerecording. She just smiled modestly and said, "A picture has to be great to be good." No one asked her to explain.

Billy had a memo from Arthur P. Jacobs, the Rogers and Cowan publicist (who later produced *Planet of the Apes*). Jacobs wrote: "I would like to point out that there are no existing pictures of Miss Monroe which can be used for publicity. She has not had a portrait sitting for two years. She is very partial to Richard Avedon, plus the fact that we feel that Avedon could capture the spirit of the 20s expertly." Marilyn had recently posed for a series of photos in which Avedon interpreted her as various stars of the past: Lillian Russell, Theda Bara, Clara Bow, Marlene Dietrich, and Jean Harlow. These were scheduled to run in *Life* magazine in the fall. Arthur Miller was writing text to go with them.

United Artists offered to fly Avedon from New York, but he was tied up. Jacobs hired a freelance photographer named Dick Miller. He worked for the syndicate called Globe Photos. When the session was supposed to begin, Marilyn walked onto the set wearing a man's flannel shirt tied at the waist and Levis. She wasn't made up and she looked distracted. When Miller started to talk to her, she waved him away. "No pictures today," was all she said before walking out.

Two days later, she submitted to the full treatment and behaved like her old self. She told me that there was nothing she liked more than posing for pictures. But I guess she had to be in the mood. She was that day. She stayed an hour longer than Dick expected. She looked sensational. At least everybody thought so. She didn't. She held up the proofs for almost two weeks before she passed a few poses for publication. She thought she looked heavy. I guess she'd read some of those snide articles. She was insecure. But with a $2 million project about to start, who wouldn't be?

It would have been a fair question to ask Marilyn: If you're frightened and you aren't enjoying this, why do it? You don't need the money. Do like Garbo. Retire. But nobody asked Marilyn, and nobody knew the truth. She needed the money.

The company she'd started with the photographer Milton Greene was not in good shape. She was on the outs with Greene. She was spending a fortune on psychiatrists and underwriting Lee Strasberg's entire operation. Arthur Miller wasn't rich. His writing wasn't bringing in as much as we thought. He had huge legal bills. In May 1957 he'd been convicted of contempt of court after refusing to tell the House Un-American Activities Committee (HUAC) the names of alleged Communist writers with whom he attended five or six meetings in New York in 1947. The case was still being appealed. He wasn't really happy with Marilyn. The reason? He knew that she was the main attraction and that she was supporting him. Poor Marilyn. Her life was in chaos. She did need the money.

In late July, Walter Mirisch heard from Lew Wasserman that he could use the title *Some Like It Hot*. As Billy Wilder prepared for the grind of production, he ran into another eminent producer, David O. Selznick, who was best known for *Gone with the Wind*. He was having a hard time in the new Hollywood. His last production, *A Farewell to Arms*, had not done well. I'd met Mr. Selznick at a number of parties. He was a complex, brilliant, intimidating man. He talked a mile a minute, jumping from topic to topic, and he had an opinion on every one. Billy sat down with him in the early summer and related the plot of *Some Like It Hot*.

"Well, what do you think?" Billy asked.

"My God!" Selznick gasped. "You start with that bloody scene? And go to men in drag? Oh, no. You can't have machine guns and dead bodies and wigs and gags—all in the same picture. You can't mix those elements. It won't work. The audience, the people, they'll walk out in droves. It'll be a disaster. You'll never make it work."

"Dave," Billy said. "I appreciate your objections. But I'm going to try it anyway."

Part IV

The Production

12

Some Like It Hot started shooting on Monday, August 4, 1958. We weren't working at the Goldwyn studio. The scene called for a train station. Goldwyn was too small to have a permanent set like that, but the MGM studios did, so on Monday morning we reported to Culver City. In this scene, Joe and Jerry come to the Chicago station to join Sweet Sue and Her Society Syncopators on their way to Florida. Although the scene doesn't occur until twenty minutes into the film, it's important for a number of reasons. It's the first scene to show the all-girl band. It's the first in which you see Joe as Josephine and Jerry as Daphne. Last, but certainly not least, it's the first scene in which Marilyn makes an appearance.

The train station set on MGM's Lot 2 looked familiar. It should have. I'd seen it in Greta Garbo's *Ninotchka* and Judy Garland's *The Clock*. Here it was with all the windows blacked out at nine in the morning, doubling for a Chicago train platform at night. Billy explained to us that our entrance was going to be a shock to the audience. No kidding. There was more, he said. Unlike *Fanfares of Love*, our film was not showing how the musicians "become" women, shaving their chests, plucking their eyebrows, and all that. All of a sudden we're at the station dressed as women—trying to "be" women. What's more, he wasn't going to have us walk into the scene. No. He started with a camera dolly rolling behind us, showing our legs as we tried to walk in high heels. Then he let us walk a bit before cutting to a front angle. That's what made him a great director. He showed the audience something that it didn't expect to see before showing it just enough of what it needed to see. No spoon-feeding, but something equally nourishing.

Jack and I had been practicing how to walk in high heels for what felt like weeks, but we were still having trouble. Billy didn't mind. "It can't be too good," he said. "It has to be kind of awkward for the audience to be in on the joke, to really get a laugh out of it." Billy later said that he added more footage of us walking to give the audience time to recover from their first laughs. If you look closely at the scene, you'll see that's true. MGM only supplied three coaches. No engine and no caboose. In the final cut Billy had us walking by the middle car over and over.

This was our first day working with the film's director of photography, Charles Lang Jr. He'd been around a long time and I'd seen quite a few of his pictures—who hadn't? *The Uninvited, The Ghost and Mrs. Muir, Sabrina.* He was a distinguished gentleman, but he always looked like he was squinting at something a long way off. That was fine with me. He made me look great, in drag and out of it.

We got our shots done and then—drum roll—it was time for the first one of Marilyn. This was around eleven. Surprisingly, she was there. In fact, she'd arrived early. "I want the world to know that Marilyn is not only on time, she is three hours early," Billy told Bob Thomas of the Associated Press. She was sitting in a chair on the sidelines, wearing a black outfit with a monkey fur trim and a feathered hat. She smiled at me, not at my outfit. She was used to that from the tests. Billy told me that she'd made a fuss when she saw hers.

"I am very disappointed," she said to him in the projection room. "I thought the picture was going to be in Technicolor. I'm at my best in color."

"Well, Marilyn," he explained, "we were fooling around with color. I tested it. It didn't look good. You know, we have these men made up as women. If we did it in color, we'd need too much makeup not to have the beard showing. It'd be a real problem. So we have to do it in black and white."

Of course it helped that Lang was a master of lighting and had gotten some lovely shots of her in the tests. But Billy later admitted that he was giving her a line. Jack and I would have photographed all right in color. We didn't look green or garish in the color tests. Billy just didn't like color. "It's like shooting inside a jukebox," he said. "Everybody looks blue or red. Even the dialogue sounds phony in a color picture."

Sitting slightly behind Marilyn on the set was a short, heavy, middle-aged woman. She was dressed in black and holding an umbrella. This was Paula Strasberg. Everyone knew who she was: Marilyn's "drama coach." There was more to it than that. The influence that Lee Strasberg had over Marilyn had to be maintained. So he and Paula flew out to L.A., rented a house in Santa Monica, and Paula followed Marilyn to the set, where she proceeded to hover over her. Literally. With the umbrella. Somebody new on the set whispered to somebody else, "Who's she?"

"The Bat," came a whispered reply. There was a precedent for the name-calling. Laurence Olivier had called Paula "the Beast" when she interfered with his directing *The Prince and the Showgirl*. There were more giggles and whispers, but Paula ignored them. Every so often, she would open her umbrella on the stage. She didn't realize how unseemly that was, how ridiculous, following Marilyn around with an umbrella—indoors. Appearances can deceive. Paula was getting $1,500 a week from United Artists. What was that for? Interpreting the script? Moral support? Keeping the sun off Marilyn? It wasn't long before we found out.

The first shot of Marilyn as Sugar was a tracking shot like the one Jack and I had done. It was straightforward and simple. The shot had no dialogue. It showed her walking along the coaches, holding her ukulele case, looking for Sue and the band. Then she passes Jack and me, and the camera stays on us as she walks off. Since we'd already walked that stretch, it was lit. The lights didn't need to be rekeyed for her. And the camera would use the same tracks to roll ahead of her.

Billy rehearsed her. She looked nervous. Her eyes darted to the side every now and then. I wondered what she was looking at. Then I saw. Paula was standing off to the side, about twenty feet behind Billy. Marilyn could see her over Billy's shoulder. That's where Marilyn was looking. It soon became obvious that as Marilyn rehearsed her walk, she looked past Billy to get

Paula's approval. There wasn't much to approve. All Marilyn had to do was walk and look ahead. When it was time for a camera rehearsal, Marilyn did the same thing. She walked the length of the platform, came past us, and then looked over at Paula, who sat there with a knowing expression on her face.

Paula's going to direct the movie, I thought. She's going to take over. Marilyn will work only if Paula says so. She's going to do only what Paula wants. How interesting is this?

Billy was ready for a take. "Action." He stepped back and let the crew move the camera along as Marilyn walked and dress extras passed by her. "Cut." Marilyn had stopped before she got to her mark, the place where she was to end the shot. Billy looked at her for a second. "All right," he said to her. "Let's do it again." I'd heard that Billy could be dictatorial and unfeeling on the set. I didn't see it. He was obviously getting resistance, but he showed no emotion. He was concentrating on the spatial components of the shot. Something was bothering him. "Action." Marilyn walked again. "Cut," said Billy. He knew what it was. He pulled the assistant director over and spoke to him. "I don't want that one," he said pointing to an extra, "crossing in front of Marilyn until she gets past this point. This is her first shot in the picture. We need to see her all the way through." He paused and looked at Lang. "Okay. Camera? Let's go. Once more, please, Marilyn."

Marilyn walked the length of the platform and craned her neck slightly. She got to the mark and stopped. "Cut," said Billy. Marilyn looked past him again, at Paula. This time he caught it. He was not going to let it go. He spun on his heel, looked Paula in the eye, and said in a very clear voice, "How was that for you, Paula?"

Everyone froze. Absolute silence. Paula sat up, cleared her throat, and answered, "Fine, Billy." He turned around and went on to the next angle. He'd put Paula in her place. And it stopped her cold. She quickly found an excuse to go to another part of Lot 2. It was a while before she reappeared. When she did, she sat where Marilyn could not make eye contact with her. Billy had fixed her. Can you blame him? He'd cowritten the script. He was the director, not some poseur. He'd staked his turf. After that,

Marilyn decided it made more sense to play by his rules. And Paula stayed out of his way.

Billy Wilder was not someone to trifle with. He was brilliant, and he had the ego to go with it. Unlike a lot of artists, he was also a businessman. He knew which end was up.

I made a mistake that first week. I came on the set while he was directing pickup shots of the girls. I wanted to ask him about billing. He was busy, but I insisted. Finally there was a break, and I asked him what size my name was going to be relative to Marilyn's and Jack's, both in the credits and on the posters. He looked me up and down. "Young man," he said. "you're quite something today. Are those pants tight or are they really pants? You look like you've been dipped in India ink from the waist down." I tried to be good natured about his joke, but I persisted with the business about my credit. It didn't sit well with him. He took a breath and gave me a look. "The problem with you, Tony, is that you're obsessed. Yes. With small pants. And big billing."

I tried to laugh. And then I let Lew Wasserman handle the billing.

13

On the second day of shooting at MGM, I did my scenes with Sweet Sue, who was played by Joan Shawlee. She'd been doing bits for years but was also known locally. She had her own club on Lankershim Boulevard. It was called Joani Presents, and it specialized in adult entertainment, talented ladies with duck's-ass haircuts wearing tuxedos and doing monologues about how women didn't need men. You get the picture. Joan was a truly talented woman with a wicked sense of humor. When she found out that she had to play her scenes against me and Jack in drag, she said, "As long as I don't have any scenes with children or animals, I'm fine." She wasn't, though. Marilyn called Billy Wilder. She had seen Joan. There was a problem. "My hair was the same color as Marilyn's," recalled Joan.

"No other blonde," said Marilyn to Billy. "I'm the only blonde in the picture." He had to concede the point. She knew photographic values. "There was a love affair between her and the camera," Billy said later. "She stood out. And she knew it."

Joan was wearing a hat in her first scene with Marilyn, so they didn't have to reshoot it, but Joan immediately reported to makeup to have her hair color analyzed. "They changed it," said Joan. "And after nine bleaches and four color experiments, almost all my hair fell out. It was seven inches long when I started. I ended up with an inch and a half. I was in danger of becoming a female Yul Brynner." She wore a wig in most of her scenes.

On the afternoon of the second day, Marilyn went to Goldwyn to look at the rushes of the first day's shooting. She sat with Billy. When the lights came up, she thought for a few minutes and then spoke to her director. "Billy," said Marilyn, "you have to come up with something more. The scene doesn't work. I'm just walking. That's no entrance." Of course, what she meant was that it was no entrance for a *star*. Billy told her that they'd reshoot it. After she went to her dressing room, I could hear her yelling at someone. "I'm not going back to the fucking film unless he reshoots my entrance! When Marilyn comes on, nobody should be looking at Tony Curtis playing Joan Crawford! They should be looking at me! Marilyn Monroe!"

Marilyn's remarks made their way to Billy. That night he met with Izzy Diamond in the office. They discussed Marilyn's entrance. Izzy brought up the much-quoted sight gag in *The Seven Year Itch*, where a burst of air from a sidewalk grate blows up Marilyn's skirt.

This meeting signaled the beginning of another phase. Though Billy was on the set every day from seven thirty in the morning to seven thirty at night, and Izzy was there, too, from this point on they were writing in the evening. There was a reason: the newness of what we were doing. It was uncharted territory. An entire picture with guys in drag. The writing had to flexible, adaptable. The project would be evolving as we filmed it, so Billy and Izzy needed evening sessions to work things out. Not to mention that the script wasn't finished. And Marilyn needed an entrance. "I couldn't sleep that night," Billy said later.

On Wednesday morning we were back at MGM. Billy had solved the problem. He had Marilyn walk beside the train again. As she passed the space between two coaches, steam shot out and goosed her. The steam was funny, even if it should have come from the engine. With comedy, you play it fast and hope no one notices things like that. But it punctuated her entrance.

On Thursday, August 7, Marilyn didn't go to MGM. She was at Goldwyn getting a ukulele lesson when a transcontinental call came to her dressing room. Her agent in New York wanted her to call Arthur Miller. The United States Court of Appeals had voted 9 to 0 to overturn his contempt of Congress conviction. He would not have to serve a thirty-day jail sentence or pay a $500 fine. The court had determined that the hearing in question had failed to tell Miller that he risked contempt for refusing to answer a question. More to the point, the court called a recess before which Miller said that he would be willing to answer the question—later. He was never recalled. But he was charged. I heard that this was payback by the HUAC for his writing a play called *The Crucible*, a thinly disguised allegory of the congressional witch hunts. Who knows? After talking to Miller for half an hour, Marilyn was so relieved that she celebrated with a solitary champagne breakfast in her dressing room.

On Friday, Marilyn invited reporters to Goldwyn so she could talk about Miller's acquittal. A dozen photographers squeezed into her dressing room as she said, "Neither my husband nor I had any doubt about the outcome of the case." While she explained this, she moved from pose to pose for the photographers. "I particularly never had any doubt because I have been studying Thomas Jefferson for years and, according to Thomas Jefferson, this case had to turn out this way." Her explanation stopped when impatient reporters asked her when Miller would be coming to see her. "He said he would probably be out before the picture ends," she answered. "I never know when to expect him. He's always surprising me. Maybe he'll even be coming this week. I don't know."

At this point Marilyn excused herself, grabbed her ukulele, and resumed practice with a coach.

People who knew the gist of the script asked me what Janet thought of my doing a picture with this sex symbol. Janet wasn't concerned. She was carrying our second child. Marilyn had a phalanx of fat women around her. Her husband was on his way. What could happen between us? Nothing. Okay, I'd been known to have affairs with my leading ladies. Not all of them. But a lot of them. It became a running gag. "Tony, do you have that in your contract?" Very funny. If I'd gone on location to Italy with Gina Lollobrigida, Janet wouldn't ask what I planned to do in the evenings. She'd ask if I was getting a percentage of the net or the gross. She had a well-organized mind, that girl. If she'd been playing Sugar in *Some Like It Hot*, it would have been a totally different experience.

14

The second week of *Some Like It Hot* took us back to the Samuel Goldwyn studio. I got into a routine. Up at seven, into the shower, into the Rolls, down the canyon to Beverly Drive, left on Santa Monica, right on Formosa, and into the parking lot. Then I'd walk across the street to the Formosa Café and have breakfast with Jack Lemmon. The eggs were tasty, and we could talk about the picture while we ate. "You know," he'd say, "I've been thinking about that scene. I have an idea." So we'd throw it back and forth. It was quiet there compared to the studio. There'd be a couple of writers at another table. And maybe some newspapermen at the bar. We knew they were hanging around, hoping to overhear something about Marilyn, so we didn't say anything they could use. After breakfast, we'd walk back across the street and go into makeup. By nine thirty, we were in costume and ready to shoot.

The scenes we were shooting that week had us in drag. One thing I discovered when I had the dress on for the tests was that the material clung and showed a lot. There was a nodule between my legs, if you get my drift. So we had to hide that. The wardrobe people gave me this steel jockstrap. It worked. I looked like one of those anatomically incorrect dolls. No nodule. No bulge. Nothing. But there was a problem. I had to wear this thing under my dress all day. When I had to pee, it was a lot of work to get this thing off from under the dress. I couldn't see myself doing this every few hours. I thought about it. What kind of mechanical thing would take care of it?

I put my thinking cap on and built a funnel-and-hose thing. It went around my thigh, down the inner side of one leg, and was hidden inside the silk stocking that I was wearing. I'd unroll it, take care of business, and then roll it up again. I didn't have to stand up or even sit down. It wasn't all that comfortable, but it worked. I should have taken out a patent on it. Nobody figured out that I had it. "That Tony!" they said. "How does he do it? In drag all day, wrapped up like a mummy. He never complains. Never goes to the bathroom. What control. What a trouper."

One day Jack caught me in the men's room. I was adjusting the thing.

"What the fuck are you doing?" he asked.

"Never mind," I answered. "I'm inventing something."

I didn't tell him because he might judge me. He was kind of conservative in an odd way.

Our first scene at Goldwyn was on Monday August 11. The set was on Stage 3. It was the ladies' lounge. Marilyn was on time and knew her lines. Billy shot the master. He worked with me and Jack and then let us go while he shot various angles of Marilyn. No over-the-shoulder shots. So I didn't see much of her that day. No one did. While Marilyn was finishing the lounge scene, a limousine pulled up outside the soundstage. Arthur Miller got out. He was dressed casually. No jacket, no tie. Just a dark polo shirt. In those days that was unusual. He came onto the stage but didn't talk to anyone. He stood by the door and waited for Marilyn to finish. Then instead of joining the company for lunch, he whisked her away in the limo.

Our first week of shooting took place on a train set across town, at the Metro-Goldwyn-Mayer studios. This scene shows me with Jack Lemmon, an uncredited player, and Dave Barry, who played Beinstock, the manager of the girls' band.

Our scenes inside the train coach were shot on a breakaway set at Goldwyn.

Here you see Jack, me, and some of the girls in the band.

People ask me if I had to compete with Jack Lemmon in front of the camera.

This is an unusual photo of Billy Wilder. He's sitting. Usually he was in motion: walking, striding, gesticulating, smoking. Never at rest.

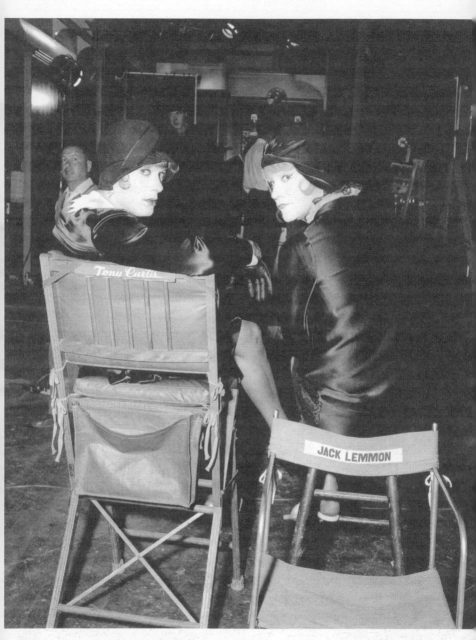

I was delighted to have Jack Lemmon as a costar. I loved the work he did. He could be theatrical without worrying if he was making a fool of himself.

With Billy Wilder, as with many other directors, I found myself looking for a father figure.

This is the scene where Marilyn had problems with bits of physical business while she was lip-syncing to the recording of "Runnin' Wild" that she'd made earlier.

Jack and I shot numerous scenes wearing high heels, standing for hours while Marilyn blew her lines. "Tony and I suffered the tortures of the damned in those heels," Jack said later.

Between takes, Jack and I
wore comfy slippers.

Between takes, Marilyn
retreated to her trailer or
consulted with her husband,
playwright Arthur Miller.

An hour later we were ready to start again. Everybody was chatty and bubbly. It was a pleasant environment. The big doors of Stage 3 were open. It was a warm day as I recall. Then the limo pulled up. A chauffeur hopped out and opened the door for Marilyn. Miller stayed in the car. When Marilyn came through the big doors, the atmosphere changed. Everybody on that stage started to quiver. She had such a reputation. Even this early, no one knew what she was going to do from one minute to the next. They almost couldn't believe she was making the picture.

Miller came in later. I had a chance to watch him. He was kind of a strange guy. He looked like Abraham Lincoln. But then all of Marilyn's husbands did. I guess she figured they knew something she didn't. But Miller was quiet that afternoon, almost glum. The stage was quiet.

The next day was a different story. Everyone in the western hemisphere had found out that Marilyn was on the Goldwyn lot. Oh, boy. It was like the Oklahoma land rush. I had a hard time parking. The Formosa Café was full by eight in the morning. There were people in and out of Stage 3 all day. We were shooting on a larger set—the interior of the coach—so they could watch Marilyn sing "Runnin' Wild" to playback. I think they made her nervous because she had a had time matching her lips to the recording she'd made a few weeks back. But she didn't tell the visitors to leave. Sometimes I saw her get huffy and do that, but not that day. As I say, with Marilyn you never knew.

I saw Maureen Stapleton on the edge of the set. She was shooting a picture called *Lonelyhearts* on the lot. "I could watch Marilyn all day," Maureen said. "She's wonderful." Montgomery Clift was in the same picture. He watched us for a while, too. He whispered to somebody, "I just want to look for a minute." He stayed for an hour. A reporter named Joe Hyams talked to Marilyn between takes. Like most of the press, he had this notion that Marilyn was making a comeback. I mean, what were they thinking? She wasn't Gloria Swanson in *Sunset Boulevard*. But people were talking like she was from another century. My God, she was thirty-two. She'd become a star only four years earlier. I'm sure her last picture was still in release somewhere.

Yet I heard this guy ask her about the difference between her and "today's new stars." I'm surprised he didn't ask her what making silent pictures was like. "I think a person is made up of a lot of things," Marilyn answered him. "As soon as you start nailing it down, you get nowhere." Ask a silly question and you get a silly answer.

Then Hyams went over and crouched on the floor next to the canvas-back chair where Paula Strasberg was sitting. And, oh, was she regal as she rolled her eyes to acknowledge him. He asked her about her work with Marilyn, but Paula could see that Billy had one ear turned in her direction, so she stuck to platitudes. "Marilyn is an extraordinary human being," said Paula. The reporter scribbled this down, nodding in agreement. "I know there are many such people," Paula intoned. "But in addition to this, Marilyn is a star. And she is one of the most gifted actresses in the world." More scribbling. "You know, my daughter Susan says, 'God put a finger on Marilyn.'" God's finger notwithstanding, it took almost two days to film this short sequence. Marilyn was beginning to have problems.

At the end of her song, Marilyn was supposed to inadvertently drop her hip flask. In the script, this causes Sweet Sue to turn sour and threaten Sugar with dismissal, but then Daphne pretends the hip flask is hers (his). Billy was shooting a medium shot of Marilyn so that the hip flask would hit the floor at the bottom of the frame. Then he could finish the shot because the scene would cut to a reverse angle of Sue. The business needed to finish the shot was not complicated, but it needed to be timed perfectly.

Marilyn had to finish the song with her arms raised. She had to let the flask slip from under her arm and land at her feet. She had to look down at the flask. Then she had to flash a guilty look at her coworkers. For a pro like Marilyn, this should have been easy. She was an excellent physical actress. She understood that part of the business. Movement, balance, timing. Unfortunately she wasn't coordinated. She'd had a hard time coming down the stairs in step with the other stars in *There's No Business Like Show Business*. It wasn't that she didn't try or care. She just couldn't get her limbs to cooperate.

Instead of sailing through this flask business—one, two, three, four—Marilyn kept messing up the sequence. In one take, she finished the song without raising her arms. In the next take, she looked around before looking down at the flask, which made no sense. In the next take, she looked down before she dropped the flask, which gave away the punch line. In the next, she lost her balance as she finished the song and didn't even get to the flask or the reaction. She couldn't seem to manage the four elements of the shot. Not to mention that she'd been singing out of sync in most of the takes. It was a little unnerving.

Billy kept his cool and worked with her, trying to reassure her. She tried again. And again.

"You aren't surprised enough, Marilyn," said Billy.

Marilyn took it again, looking more surprised but forgot to look around her.

"Cut. You still haven't got it, dear."

Marilyn looked around but couldn't see Paula.

"Don't strain for it," said Billy. "It's a very simple reaction."

Marilyn made a kind of snorting sound and stepped out of her key light. She walked over to the side of the set. Paula was there, standing with Arthur Miller. Marilyn started whispering to Paula. Billy conferred with the script clerk and then with Charles Lang. Marilyn didn't return. She stood talking with Paula. Five minutes stretched into ten, and ten into fifteen. Miller looked uncomfortable, as well he should have. He was in an awkward position. "Wilder's embarrassment was tremendous," he said later. "Wilder, as is any director, is the final authority on the set, the law. When a man is kept standing and waiting for half an hour, it's a great humiliation."

Finally Marilyn went back to her place. She started the next take, and—sure enough—she blew it. Another take. Same thing. Jack and I weren't entirely used to high heels. We were standing in this scene. Which meant that we were standing between takes, too. We couldn't go sit in our chairs. We had to be ready for Marilyn's moment. We were stuck. Well, I started to get cramps in my calves. I leaned on one of the carriage seats. "Tony and I suffered the tortures of the damned in those heels," Jack said later.

And we had to listen to that song over and over again. I heard "Runnin' Wild" in my sleep for weeks afterward. Occupational hazard.

The fact is that Marilyn never got the four things in a row in one take. By this time, Billy could see that everyone was losing his or her zip. He figured that he could do something in the editing or bring us back later, although this was supposed to be our last day on this particular set. Whatever he was thinking, he announced that there would be no more takes of this shot. All of a sudden, Marilyn perked up. "Billy," she said. "Could we try it just once more?"

No one dared to groan, but believe me, we wanted to. We did the shot one more time. She still didn't get it right. Billy did, however, take one precaution. He shot a closer angle of the flask hitting the floor. Then he let us go

15

The third and fourth weeks of shooting didn't involve Marilyn. Jack Lemmon and I had to do the scenes that open the film. There was the scene in the speakeasy, the scene in the booking agent's office, and the scenes with Pat O'Brien and George Raft. Working with men like O'Brien and Raft was a great experience for me. These were kings in their own right. They carried so much history with them. But they were down to earth. They were such good guys.

I was learning a lot about Jack. Acting is a profession of movement, never-ending movement. Jack's tempo was faster than that of most actors. He was superkinetic, like he didn't want to get caught. He talked quickly and then suddenly changed speed. Or stopped. This was a great way to emphasize something in a scene. It was so distinctive, so unusual. It became a trademark. It made him a popular leading man. Look at the women he'd worked with: Judy Holliday, Betty Grable, Rita Hayworth. These women had that extra gear that they would shift into, that made you watch them, that made them powerful. When you worked with them, you had to be prepared to move with them. Jack was doing that in *Some Like It Hot*; his energy propelling us at a whole different speed. He had a habit of saying a certain phrase when it was time for a scene. He'd say, "Magic time!" That was his mantra, I guess. Billy thought it was significant. He was impressed that Jack could capture the whole business of make-believe in two words.

Jack didn't connect with Billy right away. After two weeks, Felicia Farr asked how it was going, what Billy was like. Jack shrugged and said, "I guess he's okay." On the other hand, Billy confided to Izzy at one of their nighttime writing sessions that he was impressed by Jack's inventiveness. Billy wanted to work with Jack again, which meant creating something for him. That's how *The Apartment* came to be. Jack caught Billy's fancy. I remember a party one night where Billy said that Jack might look ordinary, but that was his gift: to portray the ordinary in an extraordinary way. He later said that Jack was an artist who could paint the Everyman. Coming from an art collector like Billy, this was rare praise.

Jack helped me improve my craft. And, of course, so did Billy. I was a quick study. I didn't want to leave it to the last minute. But because of my nighttime ramblings, sometimes I did. So I'd come onto the set mouthing the material until we got to my sequence. I was always relieved when I got my dialogue right. Some actors would blow their lines. Not me. Still, Billy found occasion to rib me. He had a certain attitude, a certain style. I wouldn't call it teasing. Provoking, maybe. He'd make little jokes. For example, when Jack and I were rehearsing a scene with him, Jack had already let go of his script. I was still holding mine. Why, I don't know. I just did. Billy needled me about that. But he never left me out in the cold.

Billy wouldn't act out a scene for you the way some directors did. Or leave you alone, like most directors did. A lot of them were traffic cops. "Come in this door. Say your line. Go out that door." That was it. They didn't care how you did it as long as you got it done on time. But not Billy. He gave you enough direction to understand the importance of the scene. And of course he and Izzy had written it. How could you go wrong? *Some Like It Hot* did a lot for my development as an actor. It wasn't enough for me to be a handsome actor, maybe the handsomest in town. It wasn't enough to learn the lines and show up. Being around artists like Jack and Billy and Marilyn affected me. I wanted to know more. I wanted to get closer to the source of the art. I wanted to know how to create that magic, like stars did in the pictures I'd seen when I was a kid. But how do you get a formula for magic?

I've heard it said that George Raft never gave a convincing line reading in his entire career. Maybe. Maybe not. But people wanted to watch him. And that's what makes a star. I'll say this for him. He was gracious all during the shooting. Billy and Izzy put an inside joke into the script. Edward G. Robinson Jr. is flipping a coin in front of George Raft, who asks him, "Where'd you pick up that stupid trick?" The joke was that George Raft's first big role was in *Scarface*, where he played a gangster who has the habit of flipping a coin over and over. It made him famous. But the joke had another dimension.

Howard Hawks had directed *Scarface*. He got the idea for the coin flipping from the great MGM producer Irving G. Thalberg, who used to do it absentmindedly while he thought up ideas for movies. Hawks's wife was named Athole. Her sister was Norma Shearer, who was married to Thalberg. After Thalberg's untimely death, Norma, who was still young, stayed single. Then she got serious about George Raft. Louis B. Mayer, the studio head, knew about George's mob connections and told Norma to break up with him. Years later, when Norma was retired, she saw a picture of a pretty girl in a ski lodge and arranged for the girl to have an MGM screen test. The girl was Janet Leigh. I never met Norma, but Janet said she was a kind woman. All this Hollywood history brought me to a soundstage in Hollywood, making a picture that Billy described as a combination of *Scarface* and *Charley's Aunt*.

George Raft couldn't do a scene the way Billy wanted it. An old character actor named George E. Stone was lying on the ground with a toothpick in his mouth. This was the scene where George has him rubbed out in a re-creation of the St. Valentine's Day Massacre. Billy wanted George to kick the toothpick out of George E.'s mouth. George E. was small, and, sorry to say, he was blind. George was uncomfortable about doing it. He didn't think it was necessary or funny. It went against his nature. Billy kept after George. "Please, please, George! Kick the toothpick!" Finally George walked off. So Billy changed pants to match George's and kicked George E. himself. He kicked him too close and too hard. They had to call an ambulance.

The scenes we shot around the exterior of the speakeasy and on the streets of Chicago were done on standing sets at MGM. When we finished, we went back to Goldwyn to rehearse our Pullman-car scenes with Marilyn and the girls. I was sitting in a chair, watching all these blondes when Marilyn walked up to me. She had a mischievous look on her face. Apparently she'd seen me looking at the girls. By that time I was a "hell of an engineer," like the old song says. She'd heard that.

"Which one do you like?" she asked me.

"Marilyn, don't do this to me."

"Go ahead," she said. "Pick one out."

"I don't want to pick one out."

"Don't you like any of them?"

"Well," I answered, "there *are* a couple there that are nice. Look, Marilyn. You know you're the only one for me."

She laughed, but she kept this up through the whole picture. It was her little joke. Nothing came of it, even though the girls were respectful to her. In fact, they were a little afraid of her. I guess they wanted to feel that their jobs were secure. Marilyn was sweet to those girls. She didn't have a lot of women friends. You couldn't call May or Paula friends. But Marilyn went out of her way to make those girls comfortable. I would see them huddled off the set, whispering and giggling.

Some girls would bring their boyfriends onto the set. I would watch them. The girls were wary. They were watching Marilyn to see what she would do. They thought she might pull their boy-friends away from them, just by using her magnetism. It got so that everything she did had some kind of significance. Regardless of polls or journalists, she was the biggest star of her time.

16

Monday, September 1, was Labor Day, so we didn't work that day. On Tuesday and Wednesday we shot our scenes in the Pullman car. I was in the lower berth. The shenanigans with Jack, Marilyn, and the girls took place in the upper berth. The set was built so that each part would break away as needed, and it was built slightly larger than a real Pullman car so that lights and everything would fit. Billy shot my angles first, but I stayed to see how they did the party. I wasn't the only one watching. A lot of people dropped in from other stages to gawk at Marilyn. Arthur Miller had gone back to New York by this time, but Paula Strasberg was there again. Some journalists were visiting, too. One of them asked Paula what she thought of our picture.

"Everything is in such good taste," she said. "It's naive purity."

I guess she didn't know that there was an office on the second floor of the Rexall Drug building on La Cienega and Beverly that worked five days a week making sure that movies were in "good taste": the Production Code Administration. If those guys hadn't approved the script, we wouldn't be shooting. But Paula was a dilettante. She knew nothing.

The same journalist came over to me and asked me about her. "I don't know why she and Marilyn go into those huddles," I said. "I guess she's helping Marilyn read her lines or something. I never saw anybody else with a coach like that on the set."

Marilyn was doing well that week. She was on time. She knew her lines. When I looked at her, she'd smile at me. When I went to my dressing room, I'd see that she was in hers. Sometimes I'd knock on her door.

"Hello, Marilyn. It's me." I'd hear an answer. So I'd ask, "Do you mind if I come in for a few minutes? I just want to sit here quietly with you before they call us."

"Of course," she'd say. "Please, sit down. Put your feet up on the hassock."

So I'd relax in there for ten or fifteen minutes while she studied her script. Sometimes—not often—we'd run lines. Usually she did that with Paula. But mostly I'd just sit there. That was it. We'd sit together until Billy called everybody. Then we'd come out. I treasured those quiet moments with Marilyn. They meant a lot to me. I could see she enjoyed them, too.

When Marilyn and I did our scenes in the ladies' lounge together, she began to look to me for support. If she was having trouble, she expected me to take her side. Her trouble became my trouble. If she felt there was too much commotion on the set, she'd look at me. I'd raise my voice. "Hey, fellas, can you keep it down? We're trying to run lines here." Once we were doing a scene and she looked at me, right in the middle of it, and said, "How's my makeup?"

"Looks good to me."

That wasn't in the script, of course. Then she went back to her lines.

Sometimes I'd come onto the set and see her in a canvas-back chair, the one with her name on it. We'd catch eyes, just like that, and keep looking. So much emotion would pass between us in those moments that I felt like I'd had a love affair with her before I even sat down.

On Wednesday Billy started the day with a master shot of her and Jack in the upper berth. It was a fairly long scene. Marilyn and Jack were both letter-perfect.

"Cut," said Billy. He turned to Charles Lang. "Camera okay?"

"Yeah."

"Sound okay?" he asked the recorder.

"Yeah."

"All right," said Billy. "That's it. Print it. Next setup."

"Oh, boy," said Marilyn. She was incredulous.

Grace Lee Whitney played a member of the band. She later became known for her work in the *Star Trek* series.

Here's a photo of
me with the girls
who played the band
members. I remember
them fondly.

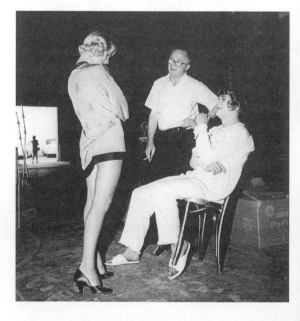

This photo shows me
and Billy talking to
Grace, possibly about
baseball, since the
Dodgers were playing
their first season in Los
Angeles that year.

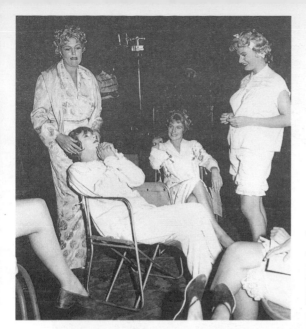

This photo shows me camping it up with Joan Shawlee, who played the bandleader. Joan had her own comedy club in the San Fernando Valley.

This is what's called a gag shot. The unit still photographer—in this case, Floyd McCarty—had to get a certain number of these during production. The newspapers loved to run pictures like these.

I wish I could recall what Joan was telling me when Floyd took this photo. I'm sure it was something funny (and dirty).

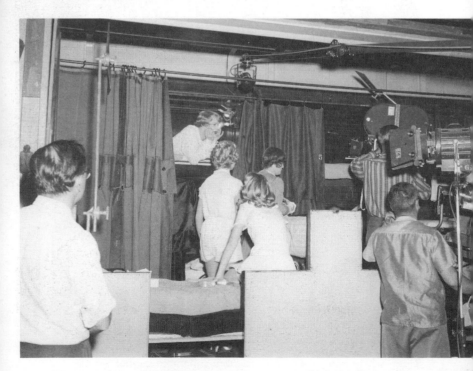

Here is a photo of Jack filming a very important close-up, the one that reminds the audience that he's a man.

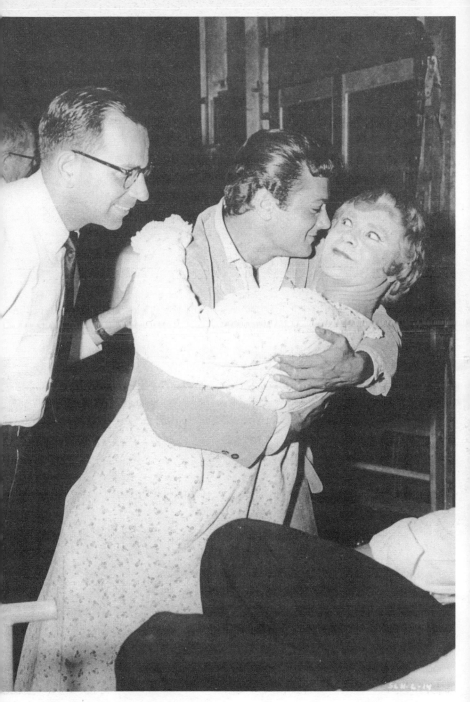

Here's a gag shot of me out of drag and Jack in drag. The odd thing is that Walter Mirisch, our producer, is also in the shot.

In real life Jack and I didn't need to be reminded that we were men. Not in that company.

Moviemaking entails a lot of waiting. You get through it as best you can. Here you see me with George Raft and Billy Wilder.

Here's a shot of our speakeasy scene. Pat O'Brien is in the foreground. Jack Lemmon and I are on the stage behind the chorus girls.

Jack and I were a great team. He never played the prima donna.

"Are you kidding?" asked Jack. "Everything was okay?"

"Yes," said Billy.

"No more takes? No other angles?"

"No," answered Billy. "You were both wonderful. Everything was terrific."

Marilyn took off while Billy shot a scene of Jack. "Billy made a closeup of me peering out from the upper berth," Jack remembered. "I had my face cupped in my hands and I was ogling the girls. Billy had played everything loose up to that point. This closeup reminded the audience that despite the female getup, this character was, after all, a man."

There was a tall, thin gentleman on the set all the time. Billy introduced him to us as Doane Harrison, his associate producer. He'd been with Billy as a film editor when he directed his first film. "He was a great help," said Billy. "He showed me in my first pictures where I should put the camera, where it would go, and where I should cut." Billy saved a lot of time by not shooting angles he wouldn't use later. It saved wear and tear on two guys in drag.

The next sequence had the girls piling, one by one, into the upper berth to join the impromptu party with Jack and Marilyn. While the shot was being lit, Marilyn didn't go to her dressing room. She sat on the edge of the berth with her legs hanging down. A journalist from the *Los Angeles Times* walked up. He was an older fellow named Philip Scheuer. I'd seen him around for years. He watched Marilyn as she started doing an odd thing. She extended her arms and began shaking her hands at the wrists. Then she put one thumb into the heel of the opposite hand and kneaded it. Then she started wringing her hands, quite forcefully.

"Is something worrying you?" Scheuer asked.

"Oh, no," replied Marilyn. "This is part of the Method. It relaxes me before I go into the scene."

"I see."

As Scheuer walked away, Marilyn resumed the exercise, but much more vigorously. Because she was perched on the edge of the berth, her balance was a little precarious. She closed her eyes and shook her hands violently. Sure enough, she lost her balance and started to fall. Luckily, one of the grips was there to catch her.

I had a bit of business where I popped my head out of the lower berth and tried to find out what the hell was going on in the upper. All I could see were a bunch of girls' legs sticking out of the curtains. Billy had me rehearse it. I got a little adventurous. Instead of pushing one pair of legs aside to look for Jack, I spread the girl's legs wide open. I forget who it was. Maybe Sandy Warner. I thought I was being cute. Billy didn't. "What if she wasn't wearing drawers?" he snapped at me. "You have to be orderly to shoot disorder." I was properly chastised.

The next scene I did with Marilyn was the one where Sugar is chopping ice in the ladies' lounge. In it, she tells Josephine (Joe) a lot about herself. It makes us care about Sugar. For all her ditziness, she's a trusting, vulnerable girl. Billy shot the master and then came in for a closer angle. Marilyn started having a little trouble with her lines. Billy had me drop a couple of the short lines that Josephine says in response to Sugar. This helped Marilyn get through the scene, and we finished that angle in about five takes. Then we shot my close-ups and Marilyn went to her dressing room. When I was finished, I went to my dressing room. I saw Paula coming out of Marilyn's. If she couldn't coach Marilyn in front of Billy, she was going to do it in Marilyn's dressing room. In a while, Marilyn went back to the set and did her close-ups.

I sensed that Marilyn felt torn between Paula and Billy. Her way of dealing with this conflict was to act. Big surprise. She was an actress, right? Well, take it from me, an actor: there are various types of acting. This was role playing. Marilyn thought she had to give each person what he or she wanted. She wasn't strong enough to say, this is who I am; take it or leave it. No. As famous and powerful as she was, she just wasn't strong enough. So she played the ding-dong for Paula, and she played the diva for Billy. That's how Marilyn was wired. I know she wasn't being difficult with Billy because of temperament. She truly wanted to do her best. But Billy came to represent a father figure for her. And that was complicated. She needed his approval and at the same time she resented needing it. There was no way that either of them could win with that kind of stuff going on. But they tried.

Everyone could see that Marilyn had an incredible gift. She was a first-rate comedienne. The way she paused and made little facial movements in the scene we did that day brought so much to those lines of dialogue. This girl is talking about herself almost apologetically. She thinks she's dumb, yet her sense of humor about it and her earnestness tell us that she's not. And the way she whacks at that ice indicates her inner strength. Marilyn made you feel that she really was Sugar, and you got an impression that there was a whole life behind her. It was lovely watching her do her scenes. As I said before, there's magic in making movies. This was part of it, watching Marilyn.

17

Our sixth week of shooting took us on location. The script described a Florida resort hotel called the Seminole-Ritz. By 1958 most of the gingerbread hotels in Florida had been torn down, so Billy had to shoot in Southern California. He chose the Hotel del Coronado, a Victorian beach resort that opened in 1888. It's about three hours south of Hollywood, in the city of Coronado, which is on a peninsula across the bay from San Diego. Charles Lang's cinematography made the white structure sparkle in the ocean air. We were using it only for exterior shots, though. Sets representing the hotel interior were being built at Goldwyn. On Monday, September 8, we took over the beach front. The first scene called for Marilyn and the girl musicians to cavort in the waves.

Word had spread through Coronado and San Diego that we'd be shooting on the beach, so Billy hired bodyguards for Marilyn and security guards to keep the gawkers out of camera range.

There were hundreds of them. The idea of three movie stars in the open air was too much to resist. The press showed up, too.

When Marilyn ran into the ocean with the girls and then emerged dripping wet, her bathing suit, dark and loose-fitting though it was, clung to her. There were remarks. One of them came from Billy. He asked Marilyn if she'd consider losing a few pounds.

"You want your audience to be able to distinguish me from Tony and Jack, don't you?" she answered. "And besides, my husband likes me plump."

Lang put up a fine black net on a frame so that the sunlight wouldn't overexpose Marilyn's hair. At this point its color was close to platinum. This "scrim" worked fine, and it helped keep people away. When it was time to record dialogue, Marilyn turned to the crowd, held up her hands, and asked them to keep quiet. You'd have thought it was Eleanor Roosevelt. They settled right down. Then Marilyn went into her Method ritual. She looked at Paula, who was sitting on the beach, still dressed in black and still carrying that umbrella. Marilyn closed her eyes and shook her hands at the wrists for a couple of minutes. There were whispered comments after the scene was shot.

"She looks like she's trying to dislocate her hands from her wrists."

"She seems scared stiff. Like this was her first picture."

"She's gotten fat. Maybe she's pregnant."

Marilyn walked over to Paula and chatted with her. A few minutes later, she did it again. And then again. "Why does she have to talk to her drama coach after every line?" asked an onlooker. "Do other actresses do the same thing?" Paula was making her influence felt, even if she was staying out of Billy's sight line. But she made sure to curry favor with him. "I've asked Marilyn not to talk to me on the set," she dissembled. "I'm only here because she feels insecure." From the way they huddled, Marilyn must have been awfully insecure.

The shots of Jack throwing a beach ball with Marilyn and the girls took most of the first day. On Tuesday, it was time for me to come onto the beach. Unlike Jack, I was not in drag. I was wearing a new costume because I was playing a new character. *Some Like It Hot* calls for Joe to have three identities. Joe the saxophone player is a peacock—opportunistic, gambling, and womanizing. Josephine, his drag persona, is a lady—sophisticated, reserved, and wary of men. Mr. Shell Oil Jr., the persona he assumes to woo Sugar, is a millionaire—privileged, sheltered, ineffectual. Playing these diverse characters required me to divide myself in three. I had to find components of these characters in my own experience. It was a challenge, but I did it, and I found it tremendously rewarding.

During rehearsals, Billy said to me, "When you dress like a millionaire and you begin your relation with Marilyn, you'll need to speak differently. You can't speak like a musician from Brooklyn. What kind of an accent can you do? Can you do a Boston accent? Or mid-Atlantic?"

This kind of bothered me. It shouldn't have, because Billy was talking about a character, not me, but it touched a nerve. After ten years in Hollywood, I was still self-conscious about my New York accent. Much had been made of it in previous years. When I appeared in one of my first hits, *Son of Ali Baba*, I had a line of dialogue that went, "Yonder in the valley of the sun is my father's castle." Some low-minded people seized on it and told the world that I had said, "Yondah lies the castle of my faddah." I was sensitive about coming from New York and being Jewish. When people laughed at that alleged line reading, they were putting down not only me but also my Jewish brothers and sisters. If you're a British actor who went to Eton, you can play a Roman emperor or a Boston Brahmin. If you're an American who went to P.S. 82, you cannot play a distinguished character. It's surprising where you find bigotry. And sad.

I thought about Billy's question. How would Joe want his new image to sound? Whose accent did I admire? Cary Grant's. After I saw him play a submarine commander in *Destination Tokyo*, I volunteered for the submarine service. Could I do a Cary Grant accent? I'd been doing that since I was a teenager.

In the scene with Sugar on the beach, I'm wearing the cap, glasses, and blazer I've stolen from Mr. Beinstock, the band manager.

I chase a defenseless child away from a wicker sun chair and his sea-shell collection. When Sugar walks by, I trip her. Who says comedy isn't fundamentally mean? After she collects herself and I apologize, she hears me. My voice is so different from Josephine—and Joe—that she doesn't recognize me. No one would.

I started with a Cary Grant accent and then I exaggerated it. I pitched the timbre of my voice a bit higher, made the accent saucy, and played with the endings of words. I extended them, made them *longaaah*. I didn't swallow the g. The British do that. I figured this guy wouldn't be smooth enough to get that. But he would emphasize the "gaaah." He'd sound not mid-Atlantic, but "mixed Atlantic." Like a charlatan. I'd met plenty of those outside the soundstages. Always dropping names, trying to sell you something. I knew the type. So I said the line—with the accent.

"Cut."

"Was that all right, Billy?"

"Great."

"But the accent?"

"What accent?

"Billy, I was doing a little bit of Cary Grant."

"If I had wanted Cary Grant to play the part, I would have gotten Cary Grant."

That was Billy. He couldn't countenance something he hadn't thought of. But he didn't tell me to stop. I would have liked a little encouragement. That wasn't Billy. It made me feel insecure.

After Sugar meets me and runs off, the script has me say, "So long." I suggested to Billy that it would be more in character for Joe to make Junior say "Cheerio!" That would be his concept of a rich guy. I was surprised that Billy let me change the line. He treated his scripts like the Bible. No one was allowed to change even a single line of dialogue. I remember the scene in Poliakoff's office, the agency where Jack and I are scrounging for work. Jack got excited, and after finishing a speech with the line "Now you're talkin'" he repeated the line. Billy froze. "That's not how the speech reads," he said. Jack pleaded. It felt right to him to say the line twice. Billy walked over to Izzy, who was sitting a short distance away. They started talking in low tones. This went on for close to half an hour. He finally came back to us. "Okay, you can repeat it," he said solemnly.

Billy wasn't picking on Jack. Billy didn't let *himself* change dialogue. He and Izzy sweated over every line, every cadence, every nuance. Izzy would add one word at the beginning of a sentence, such as *and*, just to make the sentence sound better, to balance it. This craftsmanship is what makes their pictures great.

The scene on the beach had to be shot in long takes. There were jets taking off from a naval base nearby. They made a racket every ten minutes or so. So Billy needed us to do our three-minute scene within those ten-minute intervals. Uninterrupted. Marilyn wasn't used to this kind of imperative, you might say. As vulnerable as she was, she was also spoiled. But Marilyn or no, those jets were taking off. So she had to adapt herself to the circumstances. They weren't going to adapt themselves to her.

Billy rehearsed us and quickly shot the scene. Marilyn got every word right in the first take. Billy said, "Cut. Print it." You should have seen the look on Marilyn's face. She couldn't believe it. For a second I thought she was going to faint. But no. She shook her head and scampered over to Paula, who handed her the umbrella. It wasn't hot that day, but the sun was bright. Marilyn looked kind of pale under the makeup. We didn't want her to get sunburned.

The sun was sinking. Charles Lang wanted to shoot Marilyn's close-ups with the sun backlighting her, but not so low that it shone into his lens. It was too late. Billy called it a day. We went back to the hotel. Marilyn walked there with Paula and two big guards. Her fans clapped as she walked by. She smiled at them. I got my share of attention, too. I loved it. I still do.

I never thought of acting in movies as the ultimate way of earning a living. But it became that. I got caught in that whirlpool of ambition. I wanted to be a star. I wanted everything that fame had to offer. But I learned there was more than that to being a star. I found that people were getting something from me that they didn't get elsewhere. Maybe there was something missing from their lives. I'm not sure. But I felt the affection, the warmth. Anywhere I went, I generated that excitement. I still do when I make a public appearance now. It's great to feel that I've given something to these people. But what? That quality I had. I guess I was born with it. It got me to Hollywood. But I give myself credit for doing something with that quality. I studied and practiced and trained and worked until I got to a point where I'd refined it. I could communicate it to a camera. This was my dilemma. What was I communicating? Was it me? Was it something I'd learned? Was it some magical thing coming through me? I don't know. Perhaps it's the nature of the profession. Perhaps it's the nature of human existence.

18

On Wednesday Marilyn and I shot the rest of the scene on the beach, including the part where Jack comes up and recognizes me. I loved the competition between our characters, rooted as it was in friendship and in the contrast of the guys' personalities. The story was so well written and those characters were so well etched. I've often been asked if there was any competition between Jack and me.

I had a great time working with Jack. What a sweet guy. There was never any question of competition. Never. Some actors cheat their angles, pitch their voices, do anything to make themselves look good—at your expense. Not Jack. He never played the prima donna. It was always teamwork for him. He was extremely well educated and wonderfully bright, but he never waved that Harvard background in my face. He was articulate, but he didn't spend hours telling anecdotes on the set while I was trying to get into character. He respected my process. And he had his, too. He was very critical of himself, as if he was never satisfied with what he did. Sometimes he would get so quiet. I wasn't sure what was going on. Then he'd explode into character. It was extraordinary to see.

After Billy finished Jack's shots, he worked on my close-ups. Then he called Marilyn back for hers. I watched for a while. Every so often I'd catch her looking at me and smiling. She was doing pretty well. Not too many mistakes. I started to feed her lines, and between takes we chatted. It was nice sitting there on the beach in the afternoon sun. She seemed relaxed. I looked behind me. Paula wasn't there. I asked Marilyn how she liked the hotel. She was pleasant about it. Then she leaned forward and spoke to me in a lower tone of voice. "Come and see me tonight."

That was it. Not a lot of dialogue. It wasn't like "You're so sweet. Why don't we get together? What's your room number?" That's the way I thought it would sound. No. It was just "Come and see me tonight."

I didn't see her at dinner. I had the impression that she might have left. But there was no way I could find out without being obvious. I didn't know her room number. And in those days when you were on location, where you were staying remained a secret. So I had to figure it out. And I did, or so I thought. The Hotel del Coronado was a hard place to find a room. The numbers were peculiar. There were some that were freshly painted or something. It was about ten o'clock when I went to look for her room. I went up to the floor where I figured she was staying. I looked up and down the hallway. I felt like I was in one of those silent pictures. I walked quietly up to the door. I think it was H43. I knocked on it. It opened. But Marilyn wasn't standing there. It was an actress who was playing one of the girls in the band. I said, "Hi." What else could I say?

"Hi, Tony," said the girl. "You want to come in?"

"Uh, no. I just wanted to know if you heard what time our call is tomorrow morning."

"Eight. You don't want to come in?"

"Uh, yeah, but let me come back. Okay?"

"Okay."

I knew I was in trouble. I knew that girl would tell everybody in the morning, and the next thing I'd be walking down the aisle

Jack got to go into the water in his scenes at Coronado. I didn't.

I posed for this series of photos while Billy was doing
shots of Jack and Marilyn.

Billy called me
the best-looking
kid in town. I was
thirty-three.

I never thought of acting in movies as the ultimate way of earning a living. But it became that—and more. I found that people were getting something from me that they didn't get elsewhere.

While I was on location in Coronado, my wife, Janet, brought our daughter, Kelly, to visit me. Janet was pregnant with Jamie Lee, so she didn't want to pose for pictures.

Kelly was two when these pictures were taken.

These pictures make the Hotel del Coronado look idyllic. In reality, it was a hotbe
of gossip. And I wasn't far from the center of it.

Filming *Some Like It Hot* on the beach at the Hotel del Coronado with Jack Lemmon and Marilyn Monroe was fun, but it was more than that. It was a major career breakthrough. I was working in a Billy Wilder movie.

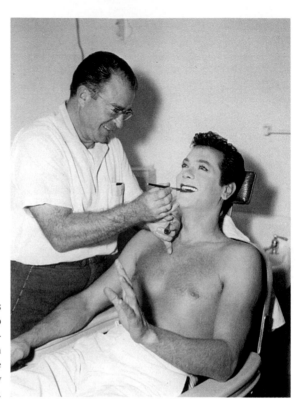

Emile LaVigne was one of the makeup artists who transformed me from the he-man movie star into a very different character.

This photo reminds me of how awkward I first felt in drag. I didn't want to come out of the makeup department at the Samuel Goldwyn studio, but Jack Lemmon (without his wig in this photo) had no fear.

Here you see me and Jack Lemmon walking from the makeup department to the stage where tests would be made of us. Billy wanted to shoot *Some Like It Hot* in black and white, and used color tests to prove his point.

This photo of me and Jack was taken during our first week of shooting. You can see us getting into character: two buddies who are always arguing.

This scene has Jack Lemmon hosting an impromptu party in his Pullman car berth. We should all be so lucky! Billy Wilder chided me that day for something I did to one of the girls who was at my eye level.

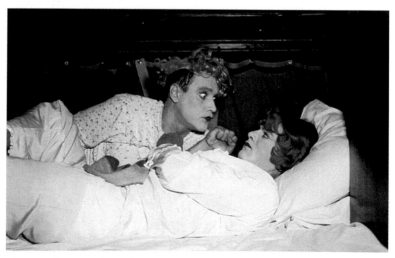

This was the scene that Billy cut after the first preview of *Some Like It Hot*. It was amusing, but it just didn't fit the train sequence.

Marilyn was in top form when we shot the Pullman car scenes. She did long scenes in one take and was a wonderful presence on the set.

Billy Wilder said that this scene between me and Jack Lemmon had the longest sustained laugh of any scene he ever shot.

Here I am waiting for a cue from Billy. This is the shot where I remember that I'm wearing the earrings from my other identity. I pull them off before Marilyn can see them.

The September weather in Coronado never got hotter than 80 degrees but was later described as 104 by parties who wanted to blame Billy Wilder for Marilyn's miscarriage.

Marilyn was very friendly during our first week in Coronado. One day I was surprised when she quietly asked me to visit her hotel room.

This photo says a lot about my relationship with Marilyn. Billy called her a puzzle without any solution. I thought she was abstract. Making love with her—on the screen or in real life—was a unique, unforgettable experience.

with her in a wedding ceremony. But I forgot about that and kept looking for Marilyn's room. Finally, by process of elimination, I found it.

Marilyn opened the door a crack. I squeezed through it. I sat down with her, made small talk, and had a drink. She wanted to talk about the movie. She was concerned about how Billy and Izzy were developing her character. I was surprised she would want to discuss this. Then I found out why she wanted to. Paula wasn't there that night. Arthur Miller was traveling. Marilyn thought she could talk to me about this. She said she wanted more scenes between me and her, more of a relationship. She was concerned about it. She was peculiar. There was no reason for her to worry about that. Billy had it all worked out in the script. I assured her that he was doing what was best for her. She seemed to accept it. Then I moved closer to her and we started to relax.

Of course I'd been with her all those years before. Now, on this night, in this hotel room, there was a feeling of two people who liked each other. And they decided that they wanted to spend the night together. It wasn't complicated. I didn't have to think about it in a complicated way. She made it simple. She could easily have pushed me away with something like, "Listen, don't come near me. You know how things are with me." She was capable of doing that. I'd heard. But she didn't do that. Quite the opposite.

When I was in bed with Marilyn, I was never sure, before, during, or after, where her mind was. She was an actress. She could play a part. She could give the part what she thought a man wanted. I never got that from her, but I never questioned her, either. I never asked for more. What I experienced with her was unforgettable.

We spent the night together. Or, rather, part of the night. I had to be up at four thirty and back in my room before anybody saw me coming out of hers. But we lay in bed for a while. We were affectionate with each other. I stroked her hair, and my hands moved all over her. Touching her, any part of her, never felt obscene or vulgar. I couldn't be vulgar with her. I didn't know what effect it might have on her. But how do you define vulgar? I didn't know. That was my problem with Marilyn. I genuinely didn't know what she wanted or didn't want. That was probably because she didn't know herself. That was her problem in the movie. She floated through it, needing someone to tell her who she was and what she was. She was both child-like and childish.

Marilyn was a child all her life. That was her way of dealing with people. It was a behavior that she used to keep them in line. I got a little of it, but not enough to hurt me. That was what she did, you see. That was what she was like. A little girl—with this incredible body. And I mean incredible. A body that had everything a man would want. She had hips like a Polish washerwoman. Not to the point that she was ungainly, but there was such a contrast between her hips and her back. She had that narrow back. And full breasts. And a long, graceful neck. She had an incredible, unique body. And she knew it. She used her sexuality.

I never could understand why she married a guy like Arthur Miller. She was intellectually unprepared for someone like that. All I could think was that maybe it was a game for her. Milton Greene was a good friend of mine, and of course he spent a lot of time with her, photographing her and even producing her pictures. She rattled him. I encountered him after he had gone to New York to see her. He was having a hard time. He wanted to be with her. He was ready to give up everything—his family, his photography business, everything—for her.

She had a lot of guys scratching at her, trying to use her. She was the most important star in movies, but she didn't really understand that. She had so much power. She could have used it in so many ways, become so great. She was hated by a lot of people, certainly by the press. There wasn't one article about our film that was wholeheartedly sympathetic to her. What they resented was her power. So much of *Some Like It Hot* rested on her. If only she'd used her power to bolster her self-confidence. But she didn't. Even as she was turning in this miraculous performance, she was losing her sense of self. And things started to go wrong.

19

On Thursday I had more scenes with Marilyn on the beach. There was no awkwardness. In fact, she didn't act as if anything had happened between us. Which was fine. I found out that Janet was coming to the set and bringing Kelly with her. The photographer Eve Arnold was there that day, too, shooting portraits of Marilyn on the beach. Janet showed up in the afternoon with Kelly. I'd finished my shots, so I got out of my costume and visited with them. I thought it would be rude to just go off with my wife and kid before they had a chance to meet everybody. But I sensed that Marilyn was getting nervous. Did she think that Janet would suspect? I don't know. But it didn't feel good, so I hung out at the edge of the set for a while, posing for Floyd McCarty, who was the unit stills photographer. Then I took Janet and Kelly into the hotel.

I didn't see Marilyn that evening. I drove back to L.A. with Janet. I later learned that Marilyn was not doing well. She stayed in her hotel room. She had May Reis type a letter to a friend named Norman Rosten. Marilyn knew him because he'd been Arthur Miller's close friend for years. She may have been drinking when she dictated the letter. She was evidently upset.

"Don't give up the ship while we're sinking," she wrote. "I have a feeling this boat is never going to dock. We're going through the Straits of Dire. It's rough and it's choppy, but why should I worry? I have no phallic symbol to lose. Marilyn." Scrawled below was a postscript. "I would have written this by hand but it's trembling."

What did she mean by that remark about "phallic symbol"? Was she referring to me and Jack playing women? Did she think that was why I went to her room the night before?

I wasn't there on Friday the twelfth, but I heard about it. Marilyn was two hours late to the set. The sun was too high to shoot by that point, so they had to wait until after lunch. Then they had to get her down from her room again. She took her time.

When she finally got back to the set, the sun was so low that they had to shoot close-ups. Jack was feeding her lines.

"It took me about two weeks to figure her out, to get used to her," Jack said later. "At first she just threw me. We'd be doing a scene, with the camera running, and she would just stop. Just like that. Whether there was one page left or one line. She'd just stop and look off and say 'Sorry.' And Billy would have to say 'Cut.' He didn't like it. No one did. But we eventually saw that she had a built-in barometer of how the thing was playing. If it didn't feel right, she couldn't make herself continue." We'd seen some of the rushes at Goldwyn the week before. "Something happens when she's in front of the camera," Jack said. "It's something between her and the lens. It's not something you can see. When I'm right next to her, looking her in the eyeballs, I can't see it. But I sit in the projection room and watch her in the rushes and there it is. A magnetism. A magic."

It was true. Marilyn had no peer at creating magic. She also had no concept of courtesy, responsibility, generosity, or of anything that you'd expect from a professional. She just had this scene going in her head and she had to get it out. Billy had been through this with her, and he thought he knew what to expect. But this was worse. I could see he was tense. He carried that tension in his back. Some people carry it in their chests or their necks or wherever. Billy stood a certain way so that it stressed him there. But I remember him saying to Doane Harrison one day, "With this girl, I'm doing many more takes than I would ordinarily. But when she finally gets the scene, yes, it's worth it."

Arthur Miller was in Roxbury, Connecticut. He and Marilyn had bought an old farm house there (his second) and were in the process of remodeling it. Marilyn was calling him every couple of days. On Friday night they talked about the feature *Life* magazine was doing with the Avedon photos of her posing as some of the old stars. Marilyn also talked about the first draft of Miller's text. She'd read it and was unhappy with what he'd written. She was so unhappy that after they ended the call, he immediately wrote a letter to her, trying to justify his ideas. He told her he was seeing a psychiatrist. He asked her to understand his mental confusion.

Marilyn tried to sleep. She couldn't. She took some sleeping pills. Maybe she couldn't see clearly. Maybe she was already groggy. She'd been drinking. She took too many pills. There was a reaction. She started vomiting. She called Paula and May. She continued vomiting. They got a doctor to her. He called a specialist. On Saturday they drove her to Hollywood and had her check into Cedars of Lebanon Hospital. The press didn't find out that she was there until Sunday. The official line was that she was undergoing tests for an illness she'd gotten in San Diego. Miller flew to Los Angeles to be with her. The production had to wait.

20

The shooting schedule for the week of September 15 had to be scrapped. There were no scenes that could be shot around Marilyn at the Hotel del Coronado. The entire company returned to L.A. and waited while Billy determined which sets at Goldwyn could be readied for shooting with other cast members.

He held meetings with Arthur Krim, Walter Mirisch, and Izzy Diamond. The possibility of replacing Marilyn was discussed. The first third of the filming was completed, but Krim asked Billy what he thought of shutting down and recasting Marilyn's part. They considered using the contingency fund. This is the percentage of a film's budget that's like the reserve tank in a car. If you get into trouble, it'll hold you over until the insurance kicks in.

I saw Billy that week and asked him what was going to happen. He said he needed to think about other options. We talked about some actresses who could play the part if Marilyn couldn't. Natalie Wood. Carroll Baker. Mitzi Gaynor. Any of them could do the part and make it work, but Marilyn had something special. Special? No. Unique. Yet Billy told me he was willing to fire her. "This is not the story of Sugar Kane," he said. "This is the story of two musicians who have to dress up like women, and one of them happens to fall in love with a beautiful girl singer."

Billy worked like crazy to line up scenes for the week. The production office was phoning everybody. They were surprised. Usually when you get a call like that, it's to tell you that you won't be shooting now. You'll have to wait. You never get a call to come in for a scene that's scheduled later in the production. By Tuesday, when Billy started rehearsing the cast at Goldwyn, Marilyn was still in the hospital. He called Lew Wasserman and asked him to speak to Marilyn and Arthur Miller. I went back to work and hoped for the best. And I hoped that Marilyn hadn't become upset and taken too many pills because of what she and I had done at the hotel a few nights before.

The Pullman set was still standing, so Billy filmed another scene of Jack and me there. In this scene, Jack sneaks from upper berth number seven to upper berth number two. This is after he's pulled the emergency brake handle and broken up the party in his berth. He climbs into number two thinking that I'm Sugar and starts to confess. I let him go far enough to hang himself and then I start to shake him "like a terrier shaking a rat." He says, "You wouldn't hit a girl, would you?" Fade out.

Next Billy was going to shoot the scenes of Daphne's date with Osgood. You know George Raft was a great dancer in his early pictures. I loved him in *Bolero*. The dance instructor on *Some Like It Hot* turned out to be kind of a dud, so George stepped in and taught Jack and Joe E. Brown to do the tango for free. George suggested to Billy that *Some Like It Hot* end with a tango between him and Marilyn. That's actors for you. I can't blame him, though. He could tango. And it would have been sensational, but not for the story that Billy and Izzy had written.

It was about this time that Billy got more bad news. Edward G. Robinson sent word that he was not going to do the picture. He didn't say why, but everyone knew. He was not going to work with George Raft, no matter how much he'd mellowed in seventeen years. Billy was livid. The only reason he'd hired Eddie Jr. was to curry favor. Now he had someone he didn't really want and he still had to cast a showy part.

I was honored to be working with Pat O'Brien (right) and George Raft (left). These men were kings in their own right.

This is a photo of the cake that turned into a practical joke on the set.

Here's a gag shot of me and Jack surrounded by the actors who played George Raft's henchmen: Mike Mazurki, Harry Wilson, Pat Comiskey, Jack McClure, and a couple of crew members whose names I can't recall.

This is a shot of Jack Lemmon and Joe E. Brown rehearsing the tango just before shooting the scene of their big date. Watching them are George Raft and the co-writer of *Some Like It Hot*, I. A. L. Diamond. "Izzy" Diamond was often on the set to assist Billy Wilder with last-minute rewrites, but they seldom took place there. Billy didn't like changing lines of dialogue on the set. The rewriting took place in evening and weekend sessions.

George Raft coached Joe E. Brown and Jack in the art of the tango. Although he's known for his tough-guy roles, George was a celebrated dancer for a time.

Here's a shot of Billy Wilder directing the nightclub scene. He used a bullhorn because there were two hundred people on the set.

Billy took his turn making the gag shot with the "gangsters," which was funny; he wa as tough as any gangster.

Walter Mirisch was disappointed and so was I. I'd really looked forward to working with Edward G. Robinson. I'd met him on the set of the Frank Sinatra picture *A Hole in the Head*. He spoke impeccable Yiddish. Like Billy, he had an extraordinary art collection. Sad to say, Eddie G. lost half of it to his wife when they divorced. That hurt, but he wanted to get free of her. He was a sensitive and thoughtful man, but those kinds of men attract unstable people.

Eddie G. was wonderful to sit and chat with. What a storyteller. He told me about his early life in New York and how he got into movies. A fascinating man, and very generous. He was impressed that I'd come up from the streets of New York. He'd squeeze my face and say, "*Shaineh ponem!*" ("Beautiful face!")

Marilyn was out the entire week. It turned out that she'd spoken to Walter Mirisch. "She was having serious personal problems," Mirisch recalled. "She asked for permission to go to New York. She was seeing a doctor in New York. So we tried to schedule around her."

We shot without Marilyn for most of the next week, too. Jack and I did a lot of scenes in hallways, and after Billy had recast the part of Little Bonaparte, we shot the gangsters' banquet scene. When I was taking classes at the New School I knew some wonderfully talented people. Bea Arthur. Walter Matthau. Nehemiah Persoff. So when I found out that Billy had cast Nicky Persoff as Bonaparte, I was happy. I think Billy was happy, too. Nicky did a great job with this one-scene role. He even shaved his head for it. But Billy was sweating the Marilyn problem. He was under a lot of stress. I felt bad for him and wondered what I could do to make him feel better. I had an idea.

The banquet scene was the gathering of the Chicago gangsters. Jack and I hide under the table while Nicky has a huge birthday cake rolled in for George Raft. After two stanzas of "For He's a Jolly Good Fellow," Edward G. Robinson Jr. pops out of the cake and shoots George and his cronies with a machine gun. While the scene was being set up, I paid a woman to surreptitiously climb into the cake—a topless stripper with big breasts. Billy returned to the set, suspecting nothing. He called "Action!"

The cake popped open. The stripper jumped out and shook her breasts. Everybody laughed—except Billy. He just stood there, slack-jawed. Somebody had topped him. "This the first time I've seen him speechless in fifteen years," whispered a crew member. A photographer from *Playboy* magazine was on the set. He tried to get Billy to pose with the stripper, but Billy shook his head and said no. I'd hoped to cheer him up, and I think he appreciated the thought, but he was too preoccupied to enjoy it.

After the joke, when Billy was filming the scene, Eddie Jr. came out of the cake and started shooting with the machine gun. He was a small guy, so the machine gun kind of took him over. He shot too wide. And Billy yelled, "Cut! Cut!" Eddie stopped. "What are you doing?" Billy asked him. "You're not going to kill the whole table, just those four men."

Jack and I were hiding under the table during this scene, but we weren't there when the wide angle was made. Our shots were done later, with the camera on the floor. Sometimes for a scene like that, the director builds a platform so that a low angle can be shot at eye level. We were already a few days behind schedule, though, so Billy just shot it on the floor even though his back was starting to bother him and he had to lie on his stomach to direct us.

The last complete scene we shot that week was the one where I'm returning from my date with Marilyn. I climb through the window of the hotel room Jack and I are sharing. Jack is lying on the bed, still in drag, holding a pair of maracas. The scene was a tricky one. On the one hand it showed the depth of the friendship these men have. They're excited to tell each other about a conquest. On the other hand, Jerry is getting carried away with the role he's playing. It scares Joe. We had to play it very deftly. There was no precedent for this in a Hollywood movie.

"Billy handed me a set of maracas," recalled Jack. "I thought he was crazy. I'd already worked out everything at home and I could not imagine what I was supposed to do with those things. As we began rehearsing it hit me. The maracas served as a bridge, a piece of business that would fill the gap between my lines."

Billy anticipated that the things Jerry blurts out to Joe would affect the audience so viscerally that, as in the case of *Ninotchka* twenty years earlier, the laughter would wipe out the next two lines of dialogue. "In the theater," said Billy, "you can wait until the laugh is over, but in film you have to guess." Jack's line "I'm engaged to Osgood" would get them going, but they'd miss his lines about Niagara Falls and Osgood's mother. "Every time I'd read a line," said Jack, "I'd follow it by waltzing around with those maracas while Tony's looking at me like I'm out of my mind." Billy timed it so the audience wouldn't miss the plot point. He'd be able to adjust it more precisely after the first preview.

At the end of the week, Marilyn reappeared. She seemed a little brighter, a little fresher. No one asked her what had happened. We just tried to get back into step. We started with the scene after the emergency brake, where she switches berths with me. Most of it was medium shots and not much business. She did fine. Billy decided that we were okay to go back to Coronado. We still had to do the day-for-night shots with the motor launch and the exterior of the hotel. On Sunday the twenty-eighth of September, they drove us down there. I didn't see Marilyn until late that night. She was arriving with Arthur Miller. And May. And Paula. They all looked kind of dour. It didn't bode well for the comedy scenes we had to do the next day.

21

On Monday September 29, *Some Like It Hot* went into its third month. I'd been on longer productions. They didn't feel as long as this one. On that day Marilyn had a nine o'clock call. Billy Wilder needed to get more shots of her on the beach. The weather couldn't have been nicer. It was going to be seventy-nine degrees. Arthur Miller would later claim that Billy had abused

Marilyn by making her run along the pier in 104-degree heat. The weather that week, especially when we were shooting at the pier with the motor launch, never got higher than eighty.

I looked down from my hotel room around eight thirty and saw the crew setting up the reflectors and the scrims and the arc lights. About an hour later, I looked outside again. They'd brought in the camera and the sound console and the boom. Billy was there with the second assistant director, John Chulay, organizing the extras. There was a crowd gathering, too, and some security officers were walking around. Somebody in the hotel must have leaked the news that we were shooting again. Then I saw Sam Nelson, the first assistant director, walk up to Billy. They talked for a few minutes. Then they both left the beach.

I had a driver take me into San Diego to do some shopping. I'd promised Kelly I'd bring her something. It must have been about one p.m. when I got back to the hotel. The crowd was larger, but something was wrong. The lights weren't on. I went upstairs and looked down from my room. They weren't shooting. I figured maybe they'd gone to lunch, although it was a little late for that. I went back downstairs and looked around the lobby. Audrey Wilder was there. I asked her what was going on. She told me that Marilyn wouldn't come to the beach. She was making excuses. First she was studying her lines. Then she was washing her hair. Paula Strasberg tried to get her to come. No dice. With all these delays, Charles Lang lost the angle of the sun that he needed to light Marilyn's close-up. So everyone was taking a long lunch. Billy had hoped that having Marilyn stay at the hotel would make it easier to get her to the set on time. Not so. She left the entire company waiting on the beach. "We got wonderful suntans while we were waiting for her," said Billy.

Finally, at two thirty, Marilyn came to the beach. She was wearing her bathing suit and a bathing cap. A security guard was walking on either side of her. The crowd started buzzing. The arc lights came on. Billy got a shot of her running from the water with Jack. Then they set up for her close-ups. Marilyn walked over to a roped-off area where there was shade from a small building. Paula was sitting in a beach chair next to Arthur Miller. She was in black,

hen I did my own stunts, Billy paid me a compliment. He compared me to Bill
olden, who'd been so athletic in *Sabrina*.

I felt that the crew was
overly concerned about
Marilyn's safety in this
scene. She wasn't going
to fall into the water. She
wasn't that dizzy.

Marilyn disliked the image
of the dumb blonde that
Twentieth Century–Fox had
sold the public. In real life
she was anything but dumb.
She and I communicated on
many levels: intellectual,
spiritual, and physical.

This famous photo shows you how an intimate scene is shot—with fifty people present. And that's just the crew. There were also hundreds of local people watching us.

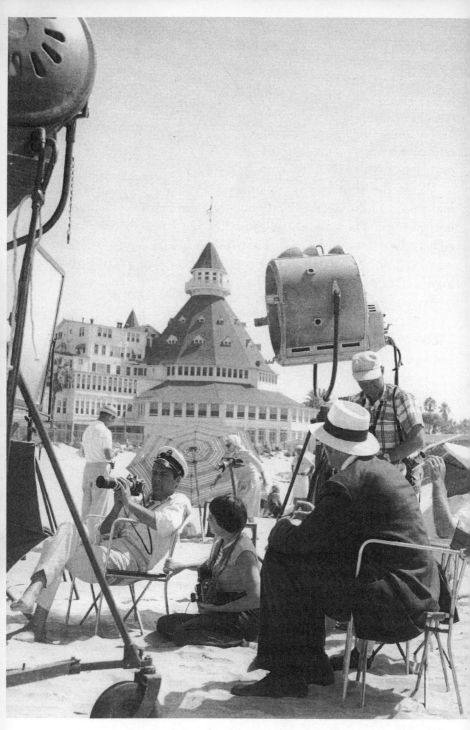

At one point during the filming of *Some Like It Hot*, a joke circulated. "What does M. M. stand for? Missing Monroe." Here I am, waiting for her to be located.

natch, but he looked more sporty than usual. He had on a striped golf shirt and an air force fatigue cap. Marilyn made him get up and give her his chair. Then she had him bring her a glass of water. You'd think she'd have had an assistant do that instead of making one of America's most important writers into a gofer. I found it embarrassing to watch. Imagine how he felt.

When the shot was ready and they pulled the stand-in, they had to send John over to Marilyn twice before she came and took her position. Then she started in with that hand-shaking routine. Billy did a camera rehearsal. They had to quiet the crowd. Then it was "Action." Marilyn couldn't remember one simple line of dialogue. "Cut."

"What did I do wrong?" asked Marilyn.

Billy read the line to her. She shook her head and looked down. "Action." Marilyn got the line out but looked the wrong way while saying it. In movie parlance, she crossed the stage line. "Cut."

"What did I do wrong?"

"Keep your eyes here. All right. Again. Action." This time she got the line, looked in the right screen direction, but there was no feeling in her voice. "Cut."

"What did I do wrong?"

"That was great, but let's try it once more."

"But what did I do wrong?"

Billy came in close and talked with her very quietly so that no one could hear. She nodded. Then he went back to the camera and they continued. This went on for sixty takes. Sixty.

Later, when Marilyn was resting between Paula and Miller, Audrey walked over and chatted with them. I knew she was inviting them to have drinks with Jack, Billy, and me at the hotel. The day's shooting wrapped in another hour. Marilyn walked to the hotel with Paula, Miller, and two guards. A hundred people trailed behind them. Paula touched Marilyn on the shoulder every so often to let her know she was behind her. The sun was, too, so she wasn't holding the umbrella over her as she usually did. Miller was wearing a fixed grin. It wasn't convincing. "There were days I could have strangled Marilyn," Billy said later. "There were wonderful days, too, when we all knew she was brilliant. But with Arthur Miller it all seemed sour. In meeting him, I at last met someone who resented Marilyn more than I did."

I got dressed for our get-together and went down to join Audrey and the rest of them. Neither Marilyn nor Arthur Miller was there. I asked Audrey what had happened. She said she'd gone to fetch Marilyn. Seems she and Miller weren't staying in the hotel. They were staying in a separate bungalow on the grounds of the Hotel del Coronado. "Pretentious," said Audrey. Cautious, I thought to myself. Anyway, Marilyn had been on her way with Audrey when Miller pulled up alongside them in a car and nodded to Marilyn. Audrey naturally had asked if Miller was coming, too. "No," said Marilyn. "I have to go." She got into Miller's car and off they went. Without saying good-bye, go to hell, nothing. Can you beat it?

The next day I was working with Marilyn. We were shooting the scene where I drop her off at the front door of the hotel after our date on the yacht. It was supposed to take place in the hours before dawn, so we were shooting on the shaded side of the building. There were lights and reflectors and everything, but the film would be "printed down" later to look like night. This was the first time I saw Marilyn wearing the white beaded gown that Orry-Kelly had designed for her. One word: wow. She had a fox stole over it, but you could see the contours of her breasts. I tried not to be obvious about it because Miller was standing on the sidelines.

Since Marilyn had been out of the hospital, she was different. She'd had her problems before, but we'd gotten the work done. She'd been friendly and chatty and available, even if she was a little distant at times. Not now. She wasn't around much. We didn't see her. It was obvious why. Miller didn't want us to see her. And he didn't want her to see us. Maybe he was afraid she'd get distracted or become infatuated with somebody.

Miller would greet me in funny ways. Odd ways. There was always a little superiority, a little hostility. To tell you the truth, he scared the shit out of me. For a while I was wondering if maybe Marilyn had blown the whistle on me. Maybe she'd told him what happened between us in the old days. Maybe she'd told him what happened in the hotel three weeks before. I couldn't be sure. I watched myself around him. And I watched Marilyn. But she kept to herself. She kept away, except when we were thrown together by the script and had to kiss each other good night in front of a hundred people.

The scene ends with Sugar going inside and Joe climbing the facade of the hotel to get back into the room he's sharing with Jerry. Billy had engaged a stuntman to do this. It would have meant cutting away from me after my scene with Marilyn. I suggested that Billy simply pan with me.

"Why don't you have me climb up to the balcony?"

"No, no," said Billy. "We can't do that. Insurance. We've hired a fellow to do it for you."

"Let me show you what I can do."

Before he could say anything more, I dashed across the veranda, leaped onto the facade of the hotel, and climbed up to the balcony. And back down again. They didn't have to use the stunt guy.

The next morning, when the sun was on the front of building, we shot the scene where the band arrives at the hotel in the shuttle bus. Because the camera was getting a wider angle, they cleared the area. It was a simple shot. Marilyn and I had to get off the bus and go up the stairs, exchanging a couple of lines. Jack was carrying our stuff, the poor guy. Billy shot several angles. Each one was difficult, not because of the content of the shot, but because of Marilyn.

First she rehearsed with us. Then she went over to Miller and Paula. They huddled and whispered. Paula touched Marilyn. Then Marilyn smiled gratefully and went back to her position. She stood there for a minute, closed her eyes, and shook her hands at the wrists. Then when she was in position, Floyd McCarty tried to get a few shots of her. United Artists needed photographs to begin selling the picture, as many as possible. Marilyn turned at the sound of the camera shutter. She gave Billy a pleading look. He looked around. "I don't want to hear any cameras clicking," he shouted. Floyd had to stop. Then, just as Marilyn was ready for a take, she heard a navy jet taking off. She closed her eyes as if she were in pain. She had to wait. Floyd started shooting again.

"No pictures," she frowned at him. "No pictures." The poor guy was just trying to do his job. But he had to stop. Marilyn had spoken.

I went to Billy and Audrey's suite Thursday night. He was being interviewed. Lloyd Shearer, the journalist, had been watching Marilyn all week. He said that he found her lacking.

"No poise, no stage presence, no savoir faire," he told Billy. "She's something of a product, isn't she? Manufactured. She has a pleasing personality, but it's the marketing professionals who have made her. She isn't a natural actress. I've watched you. You have the patience of a saint. Is she worth it?"

"I'll tell you," answered Billy. "She may have no respect for time. She may get sick frequently. She may insist upon bringing along her drama teacher. She may hold up production. But when you finally get her in front of a camera, she has a certain indefinable magic which no other actress in this business has."

"But surely she's not the only star you could cast in this film."

"I have an aunt in Vienna," smiled Billy. "She, too, is an actress. Her name is Mildred Lachen-Faber. She always comes to the set on time. She knows her lines perfectly. She never gives anyone the slightest trouble. At the box office she is worth fourteen cents. Do you get my point?"

After the interview, Billy asked me how I was doing.

"I'm having trouble sleeping," I told him.

"I'm sleeping better," he said.

"You are? How?"

Billy reached into his pocket and pulled out a box of French suppositories. He dropped four in the palm of my hand.

"What? I should use all of them?"

"No. Just one."

"It won't help."

"Slip one in your *tuchis* and you'll sleep all night. Try it."

So I did.

The next morning I came to the set. Billy asked me how the suppository worked. "I tossed and turned all night. But my ass fell asleep immediately."

I wanted to be rested. I had to leap from a pier and drive a motor launch backward without crashing into a yacht. Because of the way Billy had set up the shot, I had to do it myself. This was when I started to wonder where I stood with Billy and the company. I was starting to feel like I wasn't that important. If I got a tricky scene with lots of dialogue and business right, everybody was happy. But not as happy as they were for Jack. Or, my God, for Marilyn. That favoritism hurt me. When Marilyn got into that motor launch, they had a lot of guys standing alongside in case she fell in the water. They were overprotective of her but careless about me. That got to me.

Jack was watching all of this, but it didn't rattle him. He was a consummate performer. There wasn't much that could shake Jack from the continuity of the character he was playing. Billy didn't let anyone bother Jack. He wanted Jack to be left alone so he could get in there and do his job.

I, on the other hand, had a difficult time. I wasn't sure what I should do. I wasn't getting help from Marilyn. And Billy was spending all of his time worrying about her. I wanted to do my part. I wanted to allow myself that electricity that I've got, the speed with which I work. For example, that scene climbing the balcony. And the scene where I leap from the pier. Billy liked that. "Bill Holden was the best guy for stunts until you came along," he said to me afterward. Well, hearing him say that knocked me out—to get a compliment like that from Billy Wilder.

Of course there were other times when he complimented me. "I like what you're doing," he'd say quietly after a take. And Audrey would tell me over drinks at night, "Billy likes you very much." But he never talked about me the way he talked about Jack or Marilyn. I heard those things, and I read them. That weekend there was an article in *This Week* magazine. Billy was quoted in it. "There are very few leading ladies in the business today," he said. "Of the few, there is just one Marilyn Monroe. People go for her. She has a style that is all her own." In spite of everything that was happening, I had to agree with that.

Part V

The Problems

22

On Monday, October 6, we were back at the Goldwyn studio, shooting on the sets of the hotel interior. Most of these scenes included Marilyn. At nine a.m. Billy took Jack and me aside. "Now listen, guys," said Billy. "You'd better get it right from the first take. Get it right every time. Because the first time *she* gets it right, I'm printing it. I don't care if you've got a finger in some orifice. That's the take I'm printing."

Marilyn came to the set around ten. Not bad, considering we had a nine o'clock call. The scene we were doing was the one where we're unpacking and Sugar invites us for a swim. It was a simple setup. Not a lot of business. It should have been easy. It wasn't. Marilyn started finding fault with things. She went to her dressing room to consult with Paula. (Arthur Miller had gone back to Connecticut.) Then she asked Allan "Whitey" Snyder, her makeup man, to come in. "She'd pick up on something," Snyder said. "She'd say her eyebrows were wrong, or her lipstick. Anything to keep from going back to the set."

While we were waiting for her to come back, Billy shot the material that took place before she entered, the stuff of Jack and me conspiring. Marilyn finally returned, and we made the scene without a problem. It was funny how she could do an ensemble scene straight through without blowing a line. "Maybe it's a psychological hurdle," Billy said. "I've noticed that if she gets past the first two or three lines she sometimes can go on and on, even if it's a long speech. She doesn't seem to get tired. She'll do take after take. She poops out the other actors, but she blooms as the day goes on. She's at her best in the late afternoon, when the other actors are dropping like flies."

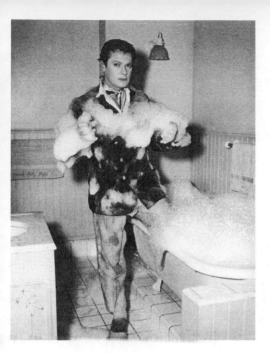

I spent a lot of time in a bubble bath, shooting my scene with Marilyn. Movie magic prevented my costume from shrinking because it had to fit me in a subsequent scene.

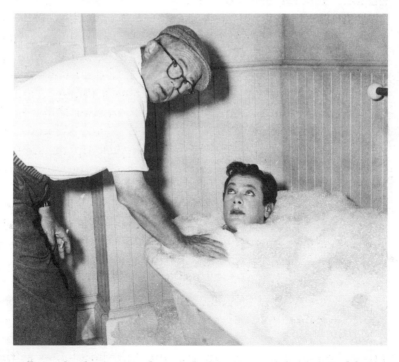

Billy tried to keep me in the mood of the scene while we waited for Marilyn to show up. I almost turned into a prune. But you can't tell it on the screen. As I say, movie magic.

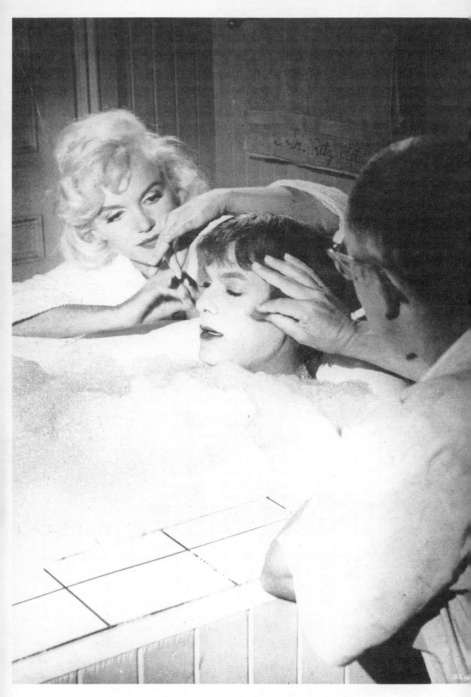

When Marilyn arrived, she proved that she was worth the wait. There was no one like her. There never will be. She had the true movie magic.

Getting Marilyn's magic onto the screen was sometimes a challenge. Sometimes a pain. Sometimes maddening. But Billy did it. We all did it.

I'd seen her last picture, *The Prince and the Showgirl*. She did long scenes where the camera kept moving and there were no cuts. She was excellent, holding her own against the great Laurence Olivier. We saw the same thing on our film. She did well in uninterrupted scenes, yet when it came to two-shots or close-ups, she suddenly lost confidence. It was odd. Billy had another theory. "Marilyn was trained at Twentieth Century–Fox, the CinemaScope studio," he explained one day. "In CinemaScope you cannot cut a scene. The screen is too wide. The scenes play much longer than they do in the old aspect ratio. Therefore you cannot cheat. Your performance cannot be created in the editing room. You have to learn the dialogue and you have to sustain a scene."

There was a short scene of me and Marilyn in the hallway outside the room, a simple two-shot. No close-ups. It should have taken a half hour to shoot. Marilyn started blowing her lines. Billy didn't raise his voice. He just said to do it again. This went on. And I saw that Marilyn was having a problem getting through the scene. She was in trouble. I had no idea why. But a pattern was emerging. She would blow a line. She would get into multiple takes. "What did I do wrong?" Then she would start crying. Then Snyder would have to redo her makeup. She'd come back. Finally she would get through the scene. Then, as soon as she finished it, she'd start crying. She was like a person who's being tortured, but not by somebody else—by herself.

On Tuesday we were shooting in Joe and Jerry's room. This was the scene where Sugar and Jerry/Daphne run back from the beach to wait for Joe/Josephine, but he's already hiding in the bathroom. Billy had given Marilyn an earlier call than usual. By this time, Walter Mirisch was monitoring her progress. "When I drove into the studio in the morning," said Mirisch, "I was in the habit of asking the guard at the gate if Marilyn had gotten there yet. Because her calls were for seven or eight, in order to get her on the set by nine. And invariably, you know, she would be in her dressing room. At eleven o'clock in the morning they would be on the set waiting for her."

It's true. Eleven thirty rolled around and Marilyn still wasn't ready. At noon word came from her dressing room. She wasn't feeling well. May had taken her temperature. She was running a slight fever. Billy asked if she could work for just a while so we could maintain some continuity with what we'd shot the day before. Her hairdresser could match her hair fairly well, but if you went too many days, it would grow, and you'd have to trim it, and there could be problems. I'd heard that her close-ups on the beach weren't matching. Doane Harrison was assembling a rough cut with Arthur Schmidt, the film's official editor. The lighting didn't match, and Marilyn's eyes looked puffy in some shots. She couldn't sleep without pills. And they caused her eyes to look puffy for part of the day.

Marilyn finally came to the set around one. She shot a scene running down the hallway with Jack. Then they did a scene in the doorway of the room, while I was behind the closed doors of the bathroom. Once again, Marilyn was fine in the sustained scene, up to and including the part where she opens the bathroom door and sees me in the bubble bath. After we got a good take, she went to Billy and told him that she really wasn't feeling well. So that was it for Tuesday.

On Wednesday, October 8, Marilyn stayed in bed at the Bel Air hotel. Her fever was 102, according to May. We couldn't shoot around her because the bubbles and all that business would be too hard to match if we shot it out of sequence. So Billy lost another day.

On Thursday we were back in the bathroom. Marilyn came to work. It took all day to get a two-minute scene of her talking to me in the bathroom. It wasn't because she was bad. She was more than good. "Marilyn was an excellent dialogue actress," Billy said. "And she automatically knew where the joke was. She did not discuss it. She knew where the laugh came. She knew." But when she was in a close-up, with the emphasis on her, the responsibility on her, something happened. I was stuck in the bubble bath. Billy was shooting past me. Marilyn started to say a line. Then she stopped. Then she started again. And stopped again. Over and over.

"Tony had his hands full with Marilyn," said Jack. "She was ill. We didn't know that until later. All we knew was that she was driving everybody nuts. You might do forty takes with Marilyn. You might do one. Billy was gonna print the one that was best for her.

I figured that out early and I made up my mind, if I let this get to me, it's going to hurt my performance."

I liked working with Jack, but I never really felt secure on *Some Like It Hot*. It had nothing to do with Jack. It was that almost all of my scenes favored him or Marilyn. I was the straight man for both of them. And I was disappointed. I was hoping this would be a breakthrough for me. It was a Billy Wilder picture, for God's sake. I mean, how much better could it get? Hitchcock? Ford? Welles?

Billy was pleasant, and, in fact, he was nice to me. But I had a way of attaching myself to people, thinking of them as older brothers or fathers. I wanted a feeling of security, of belonging, that I hadn't had as a kid. I wanted someone to look up to. But with Billy I felt like a stepson. I never felt that he really cared that much for me. Maybe it was paranoia, but that was my feeling. I talked about this to Janet. Bright girl that she was, she had an idea. Why not invite Billy and some of the major players over for dinner? Let them see you on your own turf. We invited them, and they accepted. The dinner party was set for Saturday night.

On Friday, though, we had a rough day. We were shooting the first ballroom scene at the hotel. This would feature the entire orchestra, plus Joe E. Brown and about two hundred dress extras. Marilyn would be singing "I Wanna Be Loved by You" to a playback of her own recording. We waited all morning for her. She wasn't in her dressing room. She wasn't at the Bel Air hotel. No one knew where the fuck she was. Jack and I went to lunch in the commissary on the lot. We were eating baked beans and pumpernickel. We were kidding people from the *Porgy and Bess* company, and they were kidding us. Of course they were. We were in drag. At one point I looked behind me. There was Sidney Poitier standing stock still and staring at me. I raised my eyebrows and winked at him. He shook his head and walked off. I started laughing and ordered more beans.

We went back to the set. No Marilyn. It was driving Billy crazy. He didn't know what to do. There was nothing that he *could* do, really, so he maintained his affability. He made jokes about it later. "We didn't waste those hours," he said. "We played poker. We told war stories. I managed to read *War and Peace*, *Les Misérables*, and *Hawaii*."

One day while we were waiting, Billy talked to me about a picture that he wanted to do. It would be about an American Coca-Cola salesman in West Germany. It was going to be called *One, Two, Three*. Billy was hoping to get Jimmy Cagney for it. There might be a part for me in it. But it didn't happen. I went from picture to picture. One after another. Billy couldn't wait for me. And I couldn't wait for him. Too bad.

At five, Marilyn showed up. She took her place on the set next to Joan Shawlee. She smiled at her. "Marilyn was very sweet to me," said Joan. "But she never knew who I was from one day to the next. And we worked together for three months."

Billy went over to Marilyn. "Glad you could make it."

"Oh, I know," said Marilyn. "I kind of got lost on my way here." Which was funny because Marilyn's copy of the script, the one that Paula carried around for her, had the address of the studio written on it in Marilyn's handwriting: 1041 North Formosa. We worked until eleven that night, but we got the scene.

On Saturday Janet and I hosted our dinner party. We'd invited Billy and Audrey Wilder, Jack and Felicia, Lew and Edie Wasserman, Walter and Pat Mirisch, and Jay and Judy Kanter. During the dinner, Billy was talking about the World Series that had just ended with the Yankees whipping the Braves. He was all wound up about that. Luckily it was over or Billy would have been sitting at the dinner table with a transistor radio stuck to his ear, saying "Oh, my God!" Yes, it's true. He did that. I saw it more than once.

Anyway, our dinner was in progress and Billy was holding forth on something or other. Suddenly he stopped and sucked in his breath. He was in an odd position. His face was all screwed up. He was obviously in pain. He couldn't get up. He couldn't walk. His back had just gone out.

We had to carry him into the bedroom and set him down on the bed. He was moaning. I called my doctor. Luckily he was able to come right over. He gave Billy an anti-inflammatory shot and some kind of painkiller. Everybody there felt that he was having this attack because of Marilyn.

23

On Monday, October 13, we were in the ballroom again. Billy was sitting in a hard-backed chair. He couldn't sit in a canvas-back chair and he couldn't stand. Because he'd been in the doctor's office in the morning, shooting had been scheduled for the afternoon. Marilyn's call was for eleven. We waited. She showed up around three thirty and went directly to her dressing room. We waited some more.

When I was on the set of a picture, I spent a lot of time waiting. I was used to it. It takes time to light a set and lay down tracks for the camera dolly and all that. But on this picture, I found myself—we all did—waiting a lot longer. It hurt our concentration. I'd come out of my dressing room ready to work. I'd memorized the lines, and I was ready for someone to run them with me. Sometimes it would be an actor who wasn't in the picture, someone they hired to do that. I was a bit embarrassed having to do that on this picture. I didn't feel comfortable because there I was, a guy, having to talk to another guy but acting like a woman. I wanted to feel myself going through the scene, not just mouthing words, not wasting my energy on a person who wasn't going to be in the scene with me.

In a situation like that, I found it hard to articulate the character. I needed more coaching to get me into the practical part of it. I needed to have the real actor there to give me the feeling that I would have in the scene. That's how I was able to tie the whole thing together. That's how I'd learned my craft. On the other hand, once we had a real rehearsal, shot the master and the over-the-shoulder shots, I didn't need someone there. Billy could shoot my close-ups without anyone feeding me lines. I didn't want the assistant director to go and bother Marilyn or Jack to come back just to feed me lines. I had trained myself to do without. I could draw on what we'd done already.

At four thirty Billy sent John Chulay to Marilyn's dressing room. He knocked politely. She didn't answer, but he could hear her playing records. He reported to Billy, who made no comment. At a quarter to six Sam and John handed out revised call sheets and dismissed the company. At five past six, Billy walked off the set. According to a security guard, Marilyn walked onto the set at six fifteen and was brought up short to see that there was no one there.

On Tuesday Marilyn wasn't scheduled. I had scenes in the lobby with Jack Lemmon, George Raft, and the gangsters. On Wednesday, Marilyn was scheduled to do Monday's ballroom close-ups. When she hadn't appeared by noon, Billy had the production manager call her hotel, but he got no answer. A joke started to make the rounds.

"What does 'M.M.' stand for?"

"Missing Monroe."

It was no joke to the Mirisches or to Billy. "Everybody connected with the film is burned up," publicist Tom Wood told the Associated Press. "Marilyn didn't even call in today. She just didn't show up."

Billy moved us to the bedroom set and had me do the scene where I'm talking to Marilyn on the telephone, and then I kick the box of flowers (with the diamond bracelet in it) across the hallway. That business was tricky. Try and kick a square object in a straight line. My kick was perfect the first time. I liked that.

Later when I saw the rough cut and how perfectly the kick matched her reaction shot, I got excited. These things were real to me. There was no way I could not be excited. There I was with Marilyn again. Maybe I started believing that the movie was real. This happens to me when I'm playing a part. If the situation is properly prepared, I begin to lose my identity. I'm still there, but a part of me has been taken over by the character, living in that make-believe place. I've always been thankful to the movies for that experience.

Apparently the bad press reached Marilyn. Or maybe somebody from United Artists called her. She showed up Friday, and we spent all day in the ballroom shooting both scenes. Marilyn had no problem singing to playback or with her lines, although in truth there weren't that many. But something was up. She looked a little different than she had earlier in the week. I wondered if the sleeping pills were causing her to retain fluid. She wasn't puffy, exactly. Just fleshier, if that was possible.

I was in my dressing room after lunch. I usually kept the door open in case someone needed to call me. And I liked to feel that I was part of something. If I'd closed my door, people would think that I was snooty. As I said, Marilyn had the dressing room next to mine. So I saw a lot of what was going on. And heard. The walls weren't that thick, even with the doors closed. That morning I heard Marilyn retching. When May Reis and Paula Strasberg came and went at lunch time, they looked distressed. Something was up.

Marilyn had a few more visitors. One of them was a dress extra named Sam Bagley. He was a funny old guy, given to flashy dress and eccentric behavior. The flash included a huge wad of bills. It was imposing until you looked closely. He'd put a hundred-dollar bill on top of a stack of ones. I knew Sam was a crony of Clark Gable's. There had to be a reason he was checking in with Marilyn. There was. She was trying to learn in a roundabout way if Gable was interested in working with her on the film that Arthur Miller was writing. It was interesting how stars got the "little people" to do their bidding.

After Sam left, Marilyn closed her door. I kept mine open. I didn't want them to go to her and get her to the set before I did. I wanted to show respect for her. In a short while I heard John go to her door and knock on it two times. We all knew she was in there. But she wouldn't answer the door. He kept knocking. Then I heard a murmur. Finally she cracked the door open and asked in kind of a drowsy voice, "What is it?"

Oh, come on, I thought. What *is* it? What *could* it be? The fucking soundstage is on fire?

"Uh, we're ready for you, Miss Monroe."

"Oh," she answered, and then she closed the door.

Later John came back and banged on the door. "Miss Monroe, we're waiting." Paula came up behind him and started calling through the door, too. Finally Marilyn came out and walked over to the set. "Sometimes she just would not, *could not* come out," Jack Lemmon said later. "I think she was slugging a bit of wine and stuff while she was sitting in there."

I wondered about that myself. Marilyn was getting into the habit of calling to May for a red thermos of coffee. She'd sip some and then May would take away the thermos and the paper cup. I got curious. I got one of the production assistants to check the cup. He went digging around in the wastepaper basket. Sure enough, there was vermouth in that thermos. Poor Marilyn. Why was she doing it? No one was as important as she was. Couldn't she understand the purpose of the experience? Why did it make her crazy? Why did she need some other element to make it work? Alcohol, drugs. I don't know. But in those scenes where she managed to focus herself, she was great. Somehow she kept herself from falling apart.

Back on the set, Marilyn and I did the scene where I, still in drag, kiss her on the stage in front of the entire band and then run off to escape the gangsters. Marilyn was "on" that afternoon. High voltage or wattage or however you want to describe the incredible power she had. "She was very tough to work with," said Billy. "But what you got from her—by hook or by crook—once you saw it on the screen, it was just amazing. Amazing, the *radiation* that came out of her."

Billy knew that he was getting something. And it might not last the day. He couldn't fuck around. He had to shoot as quickly as possible. So a lot of the shots of Marilyn were close-ups, and you had to hope that she matched the business of the scene from one take to the next. Sometimes she did and sometimes she didn't. You never knew. It wasn't easy for Billy or for any of us. Since we'd come back from Coronado, Marilyn had gotten obstreperous. She'd heard those remarks about her "comeback." She'd suddenly become difficult about visitors. It didn't matter if it was a member of the press, a Goldwyn studio staffer, or a member of the Mirisch family. She didn't want anyone interrupting her train of thought. Once she was in front of that camera, she could not relax.

Arthur Miller showed up that night to pick her up. It was the same deal. He hung around the periphery of the stage, unsmiling, talking to no one. When Marilyn had made her last take, Paula and May and Ann Landers, the wardrobe woman, followed her into her dressing room. Then Marilyn and her entourage headed for the alley outside the stage, where Miller was in a car. Marilyn got in and the car rolled off into the night.

24

On Saturday my phone started ringing. All of a sudden, everybody wanted to know a certain something. Even Janet asked me. The real gasser was when she handed me the phone and Hedda Hopper was on it. I could've clobbered Janet for that. But she didn't mean to aggravate me. We all had to put up with that woman.

"Tony!" came a shrill voice through the receiver. "It's Hedda. Tell me about Marilyn. Is she expecting?"

"Hedda," I answered as calmly as I could. "You know it's my Janet who's expecting. Next month."

"Come off it, Curtis. I gave you your first publicity. Don't forget that. Now tell me. Is Marilyn expecting?"

"Now how would I know that?"

"You kissed her yesterday."

"I kissed her. I didn't give her a pelvic exam."

"Look, Tony. Winchell's still got it in for you."

"And?"

"You want me to throw you to the wolves?"

"What do you mean?"

"I know about the girl in Laurel Canyon."

"Okay, okay." I looked around. Janet had gone into the next room. "All right. Marilyn's tits are enlarged. That's all I can tell you. Okay?"

"Thanks, honey." Click.

The deed was done. I hoped I wasn't the only person she'd strong-armed for her story. But she wasn't kidding about Walter Winchell. *Sweet Smell of Success*, the picture I'd done with Burt

Lancaster, was a slam at Winchell's tactics. Winchell was no longer as powerful as he'd been, but he still had the syndicated column, and he hated me. I didn't want to antagonize him.

On Monday, October 20, we went into week twelve. Until then we'd been having a fairly good time. "I have never watched a film put together in the midst of so much hilarity," wrote Jon Whitcomb, the famous artist. "During Billy Wilder's rehearsals with Tony Curtis and Jack Lemmon, electricians, scene shifters, prop men, and, in fact, the entire crew spend their time roaring with laughter."

I was delighted to have Jack as a costar. He could be theatrical without worrying if he was making a fool of himself. He was comfortable in his own skin. That giggle he did as Daphne wasn't just clever. It was inimitable. It was brilliant.

Jack didn't mention his personal life at work. We both came from a certain tradition. When you were on the job, you never discussed politics, religion, family, or sex. It just wasn't done in those days. But when I saw him at Hollywood parties, he had a glass of whiskey in his hand and he was more forthcoming. I doubt that he was ever satisfied with his performances, no matter what anyone else said about how good he was. Maybe that's why he drank after work. Not to excess, from what I saw, but he liked his cocktails. A lot of men who are gentle need to drink because they're embarrassed about not being cavemen. That's my theory, anyway.

Morale was sinking. We felt like we were reporting for duty— and with psychosomatic ailments. "Billy had to have a therapist get him out of bed in the morning," said Audrey Wilder. He was walking with a cane. "I never knew what kind of a day I was going to have," said Billy. "What kind of a character is Monroe going to be today? Will she be cooperative or obstructive? Will she explode before we get a single shot? That was the problem. I never knew." We were all on edge. And Marilyn, who had asked to work with Billy in the first place, was no longer calling him Billy. She was addressing him as Mr. Wilder. I wondered if she'd figure out who talked to Hedda Hopper. On Monday morning Marilyn arrived on time.

"Good morning, Marilyn," said Jack. "How are you?"

"Yeah," Marilyn answered blankly and walked on.

She was followed by May Reis, Paula Strasberg, Whitey Snyder, and Sydney Guilaroff, and she promptly disappeared into the makeup department. Three hours passed. What was this? Then we saw her come out of makeup. She was carrying a book I'd seen before, Thomas Paine's *The Rights of Man*. Looking straight ahead, she walked not to her chair on the set, but to her dressing room. Billy nodded to John. He followed her. She slammed the door. He got to it a few seconds later. He knocked.

"Miss Monroe. We're ready for you." Nothing. He knocked again. He could hear her locking the door. He knocked again. "Miss Monroe. It's eleven thirty and the company is waiting."

"Drop dead."

"Miss Monroe, Mr. Wilder has asked—"

"Fuck off."

John reported this exchange to Billy, who later described it as a turning point in the production. "We were in mid-flight," he said, "when we discovered there was a nut on the plane."

Part of Marilyn's snit was due to the presence of Jon Whitcomb. He'd been on the set for about a week, but Marilyn had studiously avoided him. Now word had come from Arthur Jacobs and Tom Wood that she had to cooperate—or else. So she'd taken refuge in her dressing room. Then May told her that Jon was going to do his pastel portrait of her for the cover of *Cosmo* by first taking still photos of her. Well, when she heard the word *photos*, her ears perked up. That was different. Marilyn loved being photographed by a man. For her, this was the ulti-mate aphrodisiac. It was more than that. It was a way to control someone. She needed to control every man in her sphere. She was never neutral. Depending on the man, it was either "I love him" or "I hate him." But she was incapable of ignoring a man. She had to play to each and every one.

The door of her dressing room magically opened. Jon was invited in. Then he and Marilyn emerged. She was wearing underwear and the fox stole. They headed for a hastily set-up backdrop. Floyd McCarty and a couple of grips helped with light-ing, although Jon seemed to know what he wanted. He had a pleasant manner.

"Do you have a favorite pose, Marilyn?"

"Oh, no," she cooed. "It just has to come naturally. You know, from deep inside."

"That's fine," he said. "Well, how about pretending you're Pola Negri."

"Who's that?"

"A silent picture star. Okay, let's see. I know. How about pretending you're posing for calendar art for Earl Moran."

"That's better," she laughed. "But it wasn't for Mr. Moran that I posed. It was for Tom Kelley, the photographer." She slipped the stole off one shoulder. "And it was pretty much all of me." She paused for effect. "But, you know, I needed the money."

Jon was snapping away with a Rolleiflex camera. "There's more of you now, isn't there?"

"My husband likes me this way."

"And your hair? What color is that? Is there a name for it?"

"I call it 'Pillow-slip White.'"

Jon ran out of film. Floyd reloaded for him. "What's the beauty spot?" Jon asked.

"Whitey painted it on," Marilyn answered. "It's how they wore them in the Twenties, I guess."

The session ended, and Marilyn's hair had to be reset so that she could join Jack and me in the hotel set. Jon followed her into her dressing room. The conversation turned to Arthur Miller.

"My husband says he never writes plays for any particular actor or actress," said Marilyn. "But he says if a part I can do turns up in one, I can be in it. Arthur and I bought a house in Roxbury, Connecticut. It was built around 1800, and has three hundred acres of land. About one hundred acres are in forest. I've learned how to transplant nasturtiums. He says I have a green thumb."

In about half an hour Marilyn came to the set, followed by Jon and Paula. She launched into her hand-shaking ritual. "I do it to get started," she told Jon. "An actress has to do something to get wound up. Some do one thing, some another. I shake my hands." Billy said to me that she looked like she was in a public washroom that had run out of paper towels. A few feet away, May walked up.

She was carrying the *Los Angeles Times*. She sat down next to Paula and began reading it. I remembered Hedda Hopper's column.

Jon went over to Billy. "Contrary to what you may have heard," Billy said to him, "Marilyn is absolutely tireless. She always thinks she can do a scene better than before. Her face will light up and she'll say, 'Can we do it again?'"

May folded the *Times* and handed it to Paula, who stared at it, looked around the set, and rose to her feet. Tom Wood was standing nearby. Paula walked over to him and handed him the newspaper. There was a short exchange. Billy was still talking with Jon. "It's silly to speak of this film as a comeback," said Billy. "Will Mount Kilimanjaro make a comeback?"

Tom came over to Billy, took him aside, and whispered something. Billy came back and shook Jon's hand. Jon got the point. Then, as quickly as Jon had appeared, Tom made him disappear. Billy did not want him to see what was about to happen.

25

I knew what would happen when Marilyn read Hedda Hopper's column in the *Los Angeles Times*. "Marilyn Monroe's closest friends believe she's pregnant," wrote Hedda. "If true, I hope she'll be able to carry this baby. She's been out of the picture several times, but Billy Wilder says she's so great he can forgive her anything, especially when she's not well. Jack Lemmon will be delighted to hear that Wilder thinks he has a touch of genius and that Tony Curtis is tops."

Gee, thanks, Billy, I thought to myself. And thanks, Hedda, you insufferable bitch.

The door to Marilyn's dressing room was shut. Billy, Paula, May, and Tom were inside with her. I could hear her voice, muffled though it was. "That fucking old bitch! Those cocksuckers!" Good, I thought. She's not talking about me. After a few minutes, the fulminations ceased. I heard the door open and close. I waited a decent interval and went back to the set. I had my wig on. And slippers. My feet hurt.

We were supposed to shoot two scenes where Sugar bursts into Daphne and Josephine's room. In the first, she tells them about her date with Mr. Shell Oil Jr. In the second, she tells them he's going away to South America. In movies, when there's a scene on the same set with a similar setup, it's customary to shoot them at the same time, regardless of where they occur in the story.

In 1958 a day of shooting cost $10,000. Marilyn had cost the production thirteen days, so *Some Like It Hot* was over budget. If it went too far over budget, the Mirisch Company would be in trouble. There were only so many theater seats in America. Spend too much on a movie, and even if it filled all those seats for two weeks, you wouldn't make a profit. This was the Mirisches' third movie under their new United Artists contract, and it was a crucial one. They had to prove themselves to UA. So we were doubling up.

It was almost three when we saw the slate boy getting ready. We were lit, and Marilyn had been called. Twice. Billy asked Paula to coax her into the scene. "Paula sympathized with me," Billy said later. "She was most cooperative in trying to pull the girl together." At the same time he wondered if Paula wasn't the source of the problem.

"Here you have this poor girl and all of a sudden she becomes a fabulous star," Billy observed. "So now she has all these people around her, telling her she has to be a great actress. It's too much." Marilyn finally took her position outside the hotel room door. Paula was talking to her. With all that he'd gone through since the first week of August, Billy had not lost his temper, but he did not like Paula. None of us did. In fact, I think most of us hated her. "I'm not convinced Marilyn needed training," Billy said later. "God gave her everything. Before going to the Actors Studio she was like a tightrope walker who doesn't know there was a pit she could fall into. After the Strasbergs got to her, she thought of nothing but the pit."

In this scene, Marilyn was supposed to call through the door: "It's me, Sugar." The camera was shooting past us. I was in bed, hiding my street clothes under the covers, and Jack was standing. Billy was shooting the inside of the door first. Then he would shoot an angle of Marilyn in the hallway, saying her line. He called "Action," and Jack and I said our lines. We came to Marilyn's cue. Nothing happened. "Cut." Where was she? There was an expectant silence. "We could hear Marilyn snapping her fingers nervously," Billy recalled. "She couldn't bring herself to walk through the door. She was paralyzed." We tried again. Same thing. And again.

"When you call 'Action,'" said Billy, "an actor will invariably do something. Anything. Even if it's the wrong thing. But not Marilyn. It took her twenty seconds to say a line or make a move. So to get her to come in at the right time, which is after the others are through speaking, I pressed the light button (her cue to come in) before they said their first line." She came in on cue. But she forgot to say "It's me, Sugar."

"Cut." Next take. "Action."

"Uh, it's Sugar. Me."

"Cut." Next take. "Action."

"Sugar. Me."

"Cut."

Billy calmly walked from behind the camera, over to the door, and spoke with Marilyn for a moment. He returned to his place, called for another take, and Marilyn blew it again. After twenty-six more takes, he called the prop master over. A cue card was prepared and taped to the outside door jamb. In big letters: "It's me, Sugar." On the next take, Marilyn still got it wrong.

At take forty-two, Billy walked her away from the door. He took a breath and said, "Don't worry, Marilyn."

She looked at him with a blank expression. "Don't worry about what?"

"We'll piece it together."

"I'm not worried."

"That's good. Very good." He walked back to the camera. "Okay! That's all for today."

We came back in the morning. It started again. "Sugar. Me. Sugar." After fifteen takes, she finally got it. The next setup was outside the door. It wasn't as bad. It only took twenty-three takes.

And I wasn't standing and waiting for her. I had my feet in a bucket of ice water.

In the afternoon we came back to do the other scene that takes place inside the door. We'd have done both of those in one afternoon if it wasn't for Marilyn. This scene required her to come through the door, stop, look at the chest of drawers, and say "Where's that bourbon?" Then she had to go through a couple of drawers and not find it. Then she was to walk over to where we were standing, by the end of a bed. It was a simple shot. Three words: "Where's that bourbon?"

"Action."

"Where's the bottle?"

"Cut."

"What did I do wrong?"

"The line is 'Where's that bourbon?' Once more, please. Action."

"Where's the bourbon?"

"Cut. It's 'that' bourbon."

"Sorry."

"Action."

"Where's that whiskey?"

"Cut."

"It's 'bourbon,' not 'whiskey,'" sighed Billy.

"Sorry."

"Action."

"Where's that bonbon."

"Cut. It's not candy. It's liquor. Bourbon whiskey."

"Action."

"Where's the bourbon whiskey?"

"Cut."

Three words. Three little words, as the song goes, and they were not "I love you."

"She could not get them out," remembered Jack. "Billy was going bananas. I have never seen a director come up with so many different ways to tell her how to play it after each of these takes. She'd say, 'Sorry,' and walk out the door, shaking her hands to relax her fingers."

"We've got one hundred fifty thousand feet of film of Monroe shaking her fingers," Billy told me later. I remember that they had to change the film magazine twice, just for this stupid shot. It was crazy.

"Action."

"Where's the—oh, sorry. I'll do it again."

Jack and I looked at each other and then at the slate. It said take thirty-four. I looked at his legs.

"Cramping?"

"No, thank God. Not yet. What do you think it's gonna go to?"

"Fifty," I answered."

"Ten bucks she does it in forty."

"You're on."

Billy walked over to Marilyn again and chatted with her. Paula brought her some water. Not the thermos. "All right, Marilyn. Action. 'Where's the bourbon?'"

"Where's that—wait. You said 'Where's *the* bourbon?' I thought it was *that*—"

"My mistake. Once more. Action."

"I can't," said Marilyn. "It wasn't my mistake."

"Don't mind me. I'm only the director," Billy said in a low voice.

I was in agony. My calves were crying out for mercy. Billy may have been the soul of patience. I wasn't.

"Billy," I asked, "how many fuckin' takes are we gonna do?"

"When Marilyn gets it right, that's the take I'm stopping at." If Billy was learning a lesson in patience, I was learning a lesson in humility. It wasn't an easy one.

Marilyn started to cry. Billy called Whitey to fix her makeup. And the process started again. It produced the same results. "Billy started giving her direction between takes that was incredible," Jack said later. "I never heard such brilliant direction. He dreamed up every imaginable thing to get those words out. To have her play the scene in any conceivable, legitimate way. None of it worked."

By take fifty Marilyn just came through the door and stopped. "Sorry, I have to do it again." After the next take, the bet I'd made was immaterial. I just wanted to get the fuck out of there. Everybody did—except Marilyn. "Sorry. I'll do it again."

Billy walked over to her. We held our breath.

"Marilyn," he said, "if you were just possibly to—"

"Don't talk to me now," said Marilyn, holding up her hand. "I'll forget how I want to play it."

Jack and I stared at each other. We could not believe what we'd just heard. Neither could Billy. "I have never seen a director stopped so cold," Jack said later. "Billy Wilder, the fastest mind on earth. He was absolutely stunned, and he just shook his head and walked back to the camera." Jack and I were like two bad little kids in school. We wanted to laugh out loud so badly, but we had to turn away and do it into our hands. It was fucking outrageous. Next, Billy tried putting cue cards inside the drawers. Even that didn't help. But he had to get the shot. There was no way to cut around it.

I wish I'd bet a thousand dollars on eighty takes. It took eighty-one. "I swallowed my pride," recalled Billy. "If she showed up, she delivered, and if it took eighty takes, I lived with eighty takes, because the eighty-first was very good." Cut. Print. Faint.

26

Marilyn was out sick the next day. Arthur Miller was with her. Billy stayed home, too. His back was bothering him—and his stomach. It had to be pretty bad to keep him home. Jack and I shot publicity that day. We resumed shooting on Thursday. Or, I should say, we tried to. Marilyn was ensconced in her dressing room and wouldn't come out. Walter Mirisch came to the set. He was joined by Harold. They were quite nice, asking us how we were handling the situation. Jack was honest. "I've been having this nightmare," he said. "I wake up in the middle of the night in a sweat. I'm dreaming that we're on take fifty-five. Marilyn's finally gotten her line right. But *I've* blown it." The Mirisches laughed, but the reality wasn't funny. The film's insurance might not cover the losses that these delays were causing.

Finally Marilyn came out. Billy needed the other angle of the scene that had caused so much trouble on Tuesday. "The whole idea is a laugh," said Jack. "We were called for the first shot this morning, so we arrived at 7:00 a.m. Here it is, noon, and we still haven't been in front of the cameras. They've been retaking Marilyn's scenes. How long is this gonna go on?" It was apparent to all and sundry that the production was in crisis.

"Monroe demanded take after take after take," recalled Billy. "The Strasbergs had taught her to do things again and again until she felt she got them right. Well, now she had us doing things again and again. Our nice sane budget was going up like a rocket. Our cast relations were a shambles. I was on the verge of a breakdown. She was no longer just difficult. She was impossible."

To complicate matters, Miller decided to get involved. He came to the set on Friday afternoon and took Billy aside. They adjourned to Billy's office.

"My wife is pregnant," said Miller. "Would you go easy with her, Billy, please? Could you let her go at four-thirty every day?"

"Arthur, I don't get my first shot of her until three o'clock. She has an eight o'clock call. What does she do in the mornings?"

"I was under the impression that she leaves the hotel at seven."

"She may leave the hotel at seven, but she does not arrive on this lot until eleven-thirty. She isn't ready to work until after one."

"I don't understand."

"Look, Arthur. It is now four o'clock. I haven't gotten a take."

"I'm concerned about her health in any case."

"I tell you this, Arthur. You get her here at nine o'clock, ready to work, and I'll let her go. Not at four-thirty. At noon."

Miller couldn't answer that one. Marilyn was going to do what Marilyn wanted to do, regardless of what her husband, her director, or her coworkers needed. Miller went to her dressing room. I could hear them through the door.

"You're trying the gentleman's patience," he said to her.

"What about my patience?" she screeched.

Again, Miller couldn't formulate an effective answer. How do you reason with the unreasonable? "She tried to be real," Miller

Maurice Chevalier visited Jack and me on the set of *Some Like It Hot*.

When my mother, Helen Schwartz, visited the set, she naturally gravitated to the most important chair.

Here's a picture of me with my mother, Helen, and my father, Emmanuel ("Manuel") Schwartz.

Jack Lemmon was never idle between setups.

I wasn't idle, either.

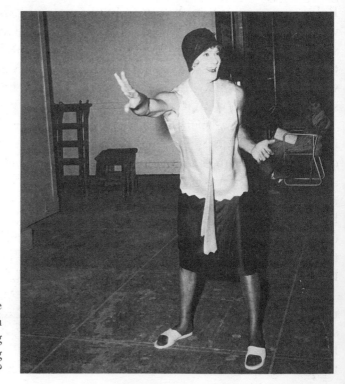

When's the
last time you
saw a drag
queen playing
softball?

wrote later. "To face enemies as enemies—Wilder was at the time an enemy—and it simply was tearing her to pieces."

The notion of Billy being an ogre like, say, Otto Preminger was a little hard to take. There were temperamental directors, yes, but not as many as there were actors. "I don't think Marilyn was temperamental," Jack said later. "She was just selfish. It was totally about her." This, from a guy who never said a negative thing about anyone. Not even about me!

I overheard Billy talking to Izzy Diamond on the set one day. The crazy hours were interfering with their evening writing sessions. "I heard there'd be days like this," Billy said. "I never heard there'd be weeks like this. I tell you, Iz, I will never work with that woman again. *As long as I live.*"

The end of production was about two weeks off, and Billy and Izzy had no ending for *Some Like It Hot.* They knew where they wanted it to finish, but they weren't sure how they were going to get there. Having Marilyn tango there with George Raft was not an option. Yet, in spite of everything, Billy and Izzy were crafting amazing scenes. When we rehearsed them, we sometimes broke up. He didn't like that. He wanted to listen to the rehearsal so he could decide if the line of dialogue, the joke, worked. If it did, he would minimize the action to make the line stand out. He knew that the wrong gesture could ruin it.

On Monday, October 27, Billy tried to finish the scenes involving Marilyn and the girls in the band. One reason for the budget overrun was that so many cast members were on call—and on salary. Joan Shawlee was particularly pleased. "Everyone else was infuriated by the delays," said Joan. "I didn't mind. Marilyn's working habits bought me a new car, a new house, furniture, and some new dresses. Besides all that, I watched her like a hawk and learned more things than I could in a drama school. The secrets of her success are her whispering voice, her helplessness, and her lack of underwear."

If Marilyn had underwear in her wardrobe from the beginning of the picture, it no longer fit. She was zaftig and then some. Her costumes had to be let out. There was also the question of poster art. It was customary for the stars of a film to pose for photographs at the completion of a film to provide images for poster design. The weight that Marilyn was gaining would make it impossible for her to fit in her costumes when she posed with me and Jack for the art. Arthur Jacobs had an idea. "Get one of the girls in the band—whoever has the same measurements as Marilyn—to pose with Tony and Jack. Then we'll cut out pictures of Marilyn's face and paste them on the girl's body." That week Jack and I posed for Floyd McCarty with Sandy Warner. Jacobs would have to worry about scheduling a photo session with Marilyn later.

As the end of production approached, Marilyn seemed to grow more skittish. Having Miller there hadn't helped. She wrote a letter to his friend Norma Rosten on the twenty-seventh. "Thank you for your Halloween wishes," she began. "It's too bad we can't be together. I might scare you. I haven't been writing anyone, let alone poems—it's so spooky here! Arthur looks well, though weaker—from holding me up. I need something to hold on to."

This was the human being that a $2 million venture was holding on to. An unnerving thought. It's a good thing that no one saw this letter. We may have suspected how fragile she was, but we wouldn't have wanted our suspicions confirmed. Not with what we had to accomplish in the next two weeks.

27

Billy Wilder had two important sequences to shoot before *Some Like It Hot* was in the can. The first was a love scene on board a yacht. The second was the last scene in the film, the denouement. The scene on the yacht has Joe dressed in a yachting cap, a blazer, and flannel slacks, pretending to be Mr. Shell Oil Jr., the owner of the yacht. Joe wants to impress Sugar. And that ain't all. He wants to seduce her. The only problem is that after masquerading as a female, the first male identity that he assumes takes on a life of its own, sort of the way that Jerry is taken over by

Daphne. To Joe's chagrin, Junior is an oil millionaire, but not a robust Texas type. Junior is an effete Ivy League type.

Billy and Izzy had set it up so that Junior takes Sugar to the yacht, but they weren't sure what was going to happen when they got them there. Who *is* sure what's going to happen on a first date? No one. That's why the boy-meets-girl scenario is worth caring about. If you knew what was gonna happen, would you watch?

Billy wanted a sex scene. At least the implication of one. You couldn't have anything approaching a sex scene in 1958 because of the Production Code. But Billy knew how to imply one. You know those devices. Door closes. Lights dim. Slow fade-out. There were all kinds of ways to convey that idea. That wasn't the problem.

"I woke up in the middle of the night," said Billy. "I was thinking, It's all set up. They're alone. Now there's going to be sex. No. This is no good. This is what's expected." So far *Some Like It Hot* had been totally unpredictable. Billy didn't want to lose that. Then he thought of something: Marilyn had been such a colossal pain. He had to make her involvement in this thing worth the trouble. The men who were coming to see her in this film, what was their fantasy? "To be subdued, seduced, and screwed by Marilyn Monroe! What could be better than that?" Nothing, except that most men would have hopped on her before she could do those things. Aha! "Most men." What if this man is more than effete? What if he's—*impotent*? "That's it!" said Billy. "Junior *plays* it impotent! And she suggests the sex. And *she* fucks *him*."

The next morning he went to his office and confronted Izzy. "Look, Iz," he said. "We are now at the situation where he takes her to the boat. There's nothing new here. But how about *this*?" This was a pivotal scene, the plot point of act two. As a plot contrivance in a Hollywood film, an impotent character was unusual. The only ones I'd ever heard of were in *Marie Antoinette*, *The Barefoot Contessa*, and *The Sun Also Rises*. But those weren't comedies. Once again, Billy Wilder was breaking ground.

Marilyn knew this scene was important. She wanted to be extra sexy. She'd be wearing the gown she wore in the nightclub scene. Orry-Kelly had given it a see-through top using the sheer silk known as nude soufflé. He'd outlined Marilyn's breasts in sequins but used sequin appliqué and extra cloth to cover her nipples. Marilyn wanted more exposure, but Orry-Kelly resisted, saying, "Sugar Kane will go only so far." Even so, the soufflé was revealing. In the shot where Marilyn is singing "I Wanna Be Loved by You," Charles Lang was using an ellipsoidal spotlight as Marilyn's key light. This was motivated by the plot: singers in 1920s bands had this kind of spotlight aimed at them. But it showed too much breast. So Lang had to narrow the beam of the spotlight and make a discreet shadow. It worked. I know there are people who write about movies and say things like "Wilder caressed Monroe's breasts with incandescent light." If that's what you think, okay. I think that all you had to do was look at her and you were caressing her. That's what eyeballs are for. We had a saying back then: "Dogs sniff. Men look."

The mood in the studio changed on the day we began to shoot the seduction scene. Marilyn was only one hour late. I was in my dressing room, made up and costumed. I heard people coming and going. Then May Reis knocked on my door and told me that Marilyn would like to invite me to her dressing room. Hmm, I thought. Interesting. I took myself over there. I was pleasantly surprised. She was smiling and relaxed. May left us alone. Marilyn asked how I was doing. There was a bottle of champagne in an ice bucket. Marilyn offered me a glass. She said we should get a little loose before we did our scene. I had one glass of champagne. It was just enough. Marilyn told me to have another if I liked, but I thought better of it. This was work, and this scene was very important.

I noticed her gown. It was really revealing. Then I realized that it looked different than it had in the ballroom scene. She had removed the pieces of cloth that covered her nipples.

"Isn't that gonna be a problem with the censor guys?" I asked.

"Oh, no," she said. "It's more . . . more organic." She was sipping another glass of champagne. "Have another one, Tony."

"Oh, I don't think so. I feel fine. How about you?"

"Oh, I don't know. I think about things."

"Like what?"

"Oh, about you."

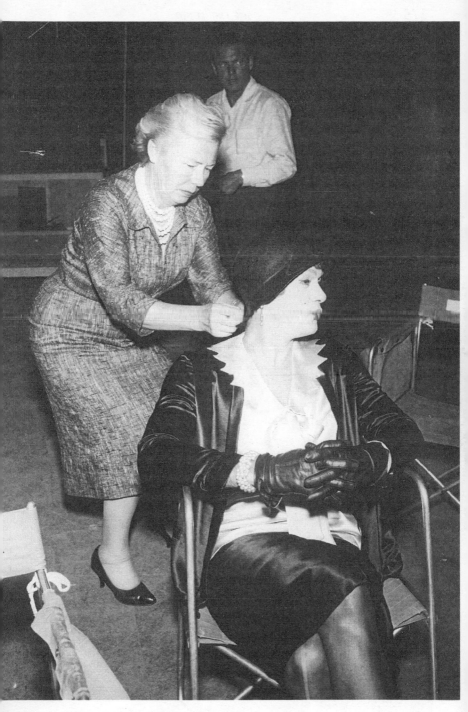

Through it all I retained my native dignity. Yeah, right.

Here's a picture of me in my dressing room. The photo was taken though my door, which was always open.

Alan Ladd visited me in my dressing room one day.

Matty Malneck was a musical director on *Some Like It Hot*. He'd known Billy from Berlin in the 1920s. He coached me and Jack.

Matty coached the girls, too. He'd been a violinist with Paul Whiteman and His Orchestra when Billy met him.

"About me? Really?"

"If only it could be like . . . like what we had before."

"You mean like at the hotel?"

"Yes."

I got up, leaned over her, and gave her a long, intimate kiss. She relaxed even more. Which was good, because we had quite a day's work ahead of us.

We reported to the set. It was an elaborate structure. There was the promenade deck of the yacht on one part of the stage. It had a pool of water next to it so that there would be highlights sparkling on us. The interior of the salon was on another part of the stage. We shot the short scene on the deck first. It was one long tracking shot done without close-ups. Marilyn had no problem with it. Then we went to the other set. This was the salon interior. It had mahogany paneling and breakaway walls so that the camera could roam around during the scene. The champagne there was not real; it was ginger ale.

In this part of the scene, Marilyn takes off her white fox stole. Charles Lang immediately saw that she'd altered her gown. He consulted with Billy, who then spoke to Paula Strasberg, who came over to Marilyn and whispered in her ear. Marilyn shook her head. Paula began to look nervous. She went back to Billy and told him that Marilyn did not want the extra cloth behind the nude soufflé. Billy called Charles, who called for some black net scrims to be placed in front of Marilyn's key light. A combination of these and a hand-cut piece of black cardboard threw strategic shadows on Marilyn's bosom. Even though Marilyn's breasts were noticeably larger than when we started the film, the scene would get by the censors. Well, that aspect of it.

To our surprise, Billy elected to shoot the kissing scene first. At the time this seemed odd. Why not shoot the script pages leading up to it first? Wouldn't it make sense to warm us up to the horizontal lovemaking? In retrospect, I can see what Billy was thinking. Marilyn had become erratic. She was unstable. He wanted to make sure that he got the most important scene in the can. Just in case. The other reason was that Arthur Miller was not visiting the set that day. Maybe he didn't want to watch what we were going to do. Maybe he had business in town. I was glad that he wouldn't be there. Try doing a love scene with Abe Lincoln watching you.

Billy cleared the set before we started. There was a reporter from *Time* magazine visiting. Even he had to go. He waved at me from the door as they were escorting him out. "Tony! Tony! Give me a quote!"

"Okay," I said, and put my hands on my hips. "Gee! Marilyn Monroe makin' love to *me*! Can ya feature it?!" I never thought they'd print it. They did. *Time* always was a snotty magazine.

The stage was set. I was lying back on the plush banquette. Marilyn was leaning over me. The scene called for her to kiss me. She did. She really did. Then the scene called for her to get on top of me. She did. Billy decided to let us play the scene in real time, even though the script called for it to crosscut with another scene, the one in which Jerry is on a date with Osgood doing the tango to "La Cumparsita." Billy would decide where to cut later. While we were on that banquette, he wanted us to live the scene we were doing. No interruptions. No distractions. No censors. Just two movie stars having sex—and enjoying it.

Well, what happened was that I got an erection, an erection that would have killed an ordinary man. And there was no way that Marilyn wouldn't notice it. She was lying on me. She hadn't expected that. It titillated her. It excited her. And it helped her do the scene. Billy kept shooting, straight through. Marilyn was pushing her mouth against mine and her tongue through my teeth. She was grinding her body against me, feeling everything. She was enjoying it. She was loving it. And Billy allowed us the privilege of doing the scene with those physical things unfolding.

When he finally in a soft and gentle voice said, "Cut," Marilyn slowly pulled away from me. She pushed herself up, looked me in the eye, and smiled. A big, satisfied smile. Like, "I got you this time, didn't I?"

28

Our next day of shooting in the salon should have been a little less exciting, a little less strenuous. You can't have fireworks every day. I didn't expect what we got. The day started quietly enough. We had a distinguished visitor. Maurice Chevalier was working on a picture with Deborah Kerr across town, but Billy wanted him to stop by now and then. Maurice had become a star in early sound pictures directed by the great Ernst Lubitsch. That man was Billy's idol. In his office, over his desk, there was a sign that read, "What Would Lubitsch Do?" Billy had cowritten screenplays for two Lubitsch films, *Bluebeard's Eighth Wife* and *Ninotchka*. He told me that he'd learned more from working with Lubitsch on those two films than from all the other directors combined. Having a Lubitsch alumnus visit the set was a thrill. And Chevalier's latest film, *Gigi*, was a hit, so we welcomed him to our set more than once.

There was another visitor that day, one whose presence was less than thrilling. Arthur Miller was sitting at the edge of the set with Paula Strasberg. They looked pretty grim. Maybe someone had told him what went on the previous day. I'd heard that Marilyn could be coquettish. Sometimes she'd flaunt her earlier affairs in a guy's face to see how he'd react. Her second husband, Joe DiMaggio, had gotten so jealous—and violent—that the marriage ended in a year. There were rumors on this set, too. Marilyn had let Miller know in her subtle way that she'd had an affair with Edward G. Robinson Jr. years earlier. When columnist James Bacon visited the set, Marilyn told her husband that she and Bacon had been "very close" at one time. And Miller must have heard about the scene I played with Marilyn the day before. This series of revelations may have been the reason for the face of granite. Or maybe that was his usual expression. He wasn't the most animated guy.

Marilyn didn't begin shooting until the afternoon. Not even Arthur Miller could get her to the studio on time, so Billy shot my close-ups in the morning. When Marilyn came on the set after lunch, she looked rested and ready. We went into the master shot where we enter the salon and then did the part where I give her a glass of champagne. That's when it started. We were two or three lines into the scene when she suddenly got a blank look in her eyes. She looked over at Paula. Then she looked at Billy. "I'm sorry," she said. "I need to do it again."

"Cut. Slate. All right. Action."

This time she got four lines into the scene. And it happened again. And again. I kept pouring the ginger ale and handing it to her. Then the prop guy would have to come over, refill and reseal the bottle, rinse out the glass, and dry it. Whitey Snyder would check Marilyn's makeup. Harry Ray would check me. And we'd do it again. The same thing would happen. At least I wasn't wearing high heels this time. But it was aggravating.

"Marilyn had a kind of built in alarm system," said Jack Lemmon. "It would go off in the middle of a scene if it wasn't right for her, and she would stop. It would look like she was doing exactly what she'd done in the previous take. But for her, something wasn't clicking. She knew she was limited. She knew what was right for Marilyn. She wasn't about to do anything else. So she'd stand there with her eyes closed, biting her lip, and wringing her hands until she had it worked out."

And I stood there with this glass of ginger ale in my hand, wondering if she was brilliant or just selfish. "She didn't mean to be selfish," Jack told me later. "It was the only way she could work. Marilyn didn't give a rip about the director, or the other actors, or anything else. She had to get that scene the way she pictured it in her head." And he added, "I know it drove you cuckoo." Indeed it did. I've rarely lost my temper on a motion picture set. But I did that day.

At take thirty-eight I was handing her the glass of "champagne." I had done it so many times that I was numb, moving like a robot. Marilyn stopped in the middle of the scene, just as the glass was going into her hand. I snapped. I pushed the glass at her. She deflected it. It went flying. Miller jumped up and ran over to us. He pushed me. I pushed him back. He tripped and fell. Marilyn came at me. I pushed her away. Billy and John and Sam rushed over and separated everybody. Billy called a break. I went to my dressing room.

About a half hour later, I heard arguing coming from Marilyn's dressing room. It sounded like Miller was yelling at her. "What else is there? Tell me." Then it quieted down. Another half hour passed. There was a knock on my door. Arthur Jacobs was there. He came in and asked if I was all right. Would I be amenable to talking with Marilyn and her husband, in order to smooth things over? Of course I would. I didn't want to be on bad terms with anyone. As I said, the big thing in my life has been that I so much want people to like me. So I said I'd talk with them. Jacobs left. A few minutes later, he came back and escorted me to Marilyn's dressing room. Miller was there, of course, and Marilyn, but no May Reis or Paula Strasberg.

I stepped inside. Miller looked distinctly ill at ease. Marilyn was staring into space.

"Marilyn, Arthur," I began. "I'm sorry. I've been . . . we've all been through the wringer. We're all tired. I didn't mean anything. Please accept my apology." I extended my hand.

Marilyn looked up and nodded. Miller turned to Jacobs. "We'd like to speak to Mr. Curtis alone."

Jacobs looked frightened. This was coming out of nowhere. "Very well," he said. Then he backed out of the dressing room and closed the door.

I turned to Miller. "What? You don't want to accept my apology?"

"If you'll apologize for sleeping with my wife," he said, glaring at me. Marilyn looked down at the floor.

"What?" I gulped. What the fuck was this? This was something I hadn't expected

"She told me about the hotel," Miller said flatly.

"Oh," I answered. "Okay." I suddenly felt weird. There was a heaviness in my chest and arms. I tried to breathe.

"Well?" asked Miller, lifting his chin.

I looked at Marilyn, then back at him. My mouth was dry. "Look," I said, taking a breath. "Okay. I'm sorry. I really am. But you have to understand. Marilyn and I have a special feeling for each other. It started long before you came around. When we were together, it came back. I'm sorry."

"Is this true?" he asked her.

"Yes," she answered, looking down.

"This should not have happened," he said, pushing his glasses up on his nose.

"Well," I said, "it did. We didn't want to do this to you. But it just . . . happened. And I'm sorry. Very sorry."

"Sorry?" asked Miller. "What good does that do us? You Hollywood people are so incredibly selfish."

"Look. Don't blame Hollywood. Like I said. It just happened. There's nothing we can do about it now."

"There's something I can do about it," said Miller. "I can beat the hell out of you."

This guy was full of shit. He didn't know who the fuck he was dealing with. I crossed my arms. "Yeah?"

"Stop it," said Marilyn. She stood up and put her hand on his arm. "That won't fix it."

"What's to fix?" I asked her.

"There's something I—" She looked from me to him and back again.

"Don't," he cut her off. He stepped in front of her. They stood staring at each other.

Then she stepped back and looked at me. "I think the baby is yours," said Marilyn.

"What?" I couldn't say anything else. I was stunned. My head started buzzing. I just stood there. The room was silent. I could hear tires screeching on Santa Monica Boulevard.

"We've discussed that," Miller said to her. "It's not his."

"Fine," said Marilyn. "It's not his. Fine. Whatever you say."

"What makes you think the baby is mine?" I asked.

"Nothing," said Miller. "Nothing."

"Are you serious, Marilyn? Is it—"

"I've consulted her doctor," Miller cut in. "There's no way it could be yours."

"Look," I said, "I'm sorry. What do you want me to do?"

"There's nothing for you to do." Marilyn slumped back into her chair.

"What do you want me to do?" I asked again.

"Finish the film," said Miller. "And stay out of our lives."

I stared at him for a minute. Then I looked at her. She was crying. "Okay," I said. "That I can do." I turned and walked out. I went to my dressing room. I closed the door. I locked it.

Billy sent everyone home for the day. The next day Marilyn called in sick. I knew why. Walter Winchell had finally gotten back at me for *Sweet Smell of Success*. He wrote a nasty item in his column about my getting into a fistfight with Arthur Miller *and* Marilyn Monroe. Interesting how news travels in the jungle.

On Friday morning Marilyn was on the set early. Miller was not there at all. We took up where we'd left off, with the champagne. She got it on the first take. Then we did the part where I'm chewing on a pheasant leg. Only it was chicken, because it would photograph better. Pheasant is too gamy to last under the lights.

Marilyn began doing it again. Starting and stopping. We went to forty-two takes. By the last take I was turning eight shades of chartreuse. I was ready to throw up. I didn't eat chicken for a long time after that.

29

On Monday, November 3, *Some Like It Hot* went into its fourteenth week of shooting. Billy Wilder and I. A. L. Diamond had not completed the script. They were still grappling with it. In the meantime there were shots to be gotten. Marilyn and Jack and I spent most of the day running around hallways or talking on telephones in close-ups that had to be reshot for one reason or another. Fortunately, as we got closer to the end, Marilyn was able to get a shot in fewer takes. Some of them were just reaction shots, of course. And she was reading her lines off blackboards positioned just out of camera range. Billy tried to get her not to scan her eyes from left to right, but she did it anyway. You could tell she was reading, especially in the shot when she's on the phone.

We spent quite a bit of time on the process stage. That's where they film you in front of a translucent rear projection screen and you pretend you're somewhere else. We had a number of those shots to do, where I was riding a bicycle, for example. We closed down fairly early. There was a good reason. Billy needed to sit down with Izzy and write the ending of our movie. Before they adjourned to the office, though, they screened rushes from the previous week's shooting.

I was curious to see how my love scene with Marilyn looked. When I got to the screening room, I was surprised. There were people there who shouldn't have been: publicists and crew members from other productions. I wanted to ask Billy if he could send them away, but I didn't see him. The lights dimmed. The projector started rolling. Various takes were projected onto the screen. They looked good at first. But then I realized that the takes Billy had printed were the ones where Marilyn was warming up—and I was wearing down. This I did not like.

What I also didn't like was the undercurrent of crudeness in the screening room, as if this was a smoker, not a private screening of a work in progress—a very important work. There were remarks of a vulgar nature about Marilyn's breasts and about the way she was on top of me. I was getting hot under the collar. But Billy didn't come in until after the screening had started. I couldn't very well tell him to turn off the projector and throw the punks out.

The lights came up. I had to leave. On my way out, some guy whom I didn't recognize called out to me.

"Tony," he said. "That was terrific. Hey. Tell me. What was it like kissing Marilyn?"

I didn't stop to acknowledge him. I kept walking.

"What do you think it was like, buddy?" I got to the door. "Like kissing Hitler?"

I went through the door and slammed it after me.

30

Billy Wilder didn't care what I'd said about Marilyn in the screening room. He had more pressing concerns, like his health.

His back had gotten better, but now his stomach was bothering him. He'd been vomiting from sheer stress. Marilyn wasn't the only reason. The ending for the film had yet to be written. This was standard procedure for Billy and Izzy. They always wrote their scripts as shooting progressed. The actors informed the characters, and the characters informed the plot. Billy didn't usually cut it so close. On Monday after screening the rushes, he joined Izzy in the office and tried to thrash out the last scene.

They'd gotten our heroes (or were they heroines?) safely away from the gangsters and into that motor launch: Joe is in the back seat with Sugar, and Jerry is in the front seat with Osgood. It was a given that Sugar would accept Joe, even though he was a no-good saxophone player. But how the hell was Osgood going to react when he found out Daphne was really Jerry? Billy and Izzy had painted themselves into a corner. Or had they?

In the earlier scene where I climb through the window into the hotel room and Jack uses the maracas to punctuate his pronouncements, I had the line, "How can you marry Osgood? You're not a girl. You're a guy!" Jack's next line was originally, "Nobody's perfect." Billy thought that it broke the continuity and called attention to itself. He and Izzy acted out the scene so they could hear the rhythm. As funny as this line was, it didn't belong in that rapid-fire scene. So they cut it.

Weeks later, on Monday, November 3, Billy was playing the very last scene with Izzy.

"And Jerry takes off his wig and says, 'But you don't understand. I'm a man!'"

"Well . . . nobody's perfect," Izzy said, almost devoid of emotion.

"What's that?" asked Billy. "A throwaway?"

"I don't know. Why don't we use it?"

Billy wasn't sure. But he couldn't think of anything better. Still, there might be something.

"It's getting late," said Izzy. "If we play with this much longer, we won't be able to get it typed and mimeographed tonight." The production office closed at nine.

"Well . . . all right," Billy said. "Let's put it in. But just for the time being. We've got 'til Friday to think of something else." Izzy

This picture was taken on the last day I worked with Marilyn
Monroe. It was on the process stage at Goldwyn. I thought I'd see
her the next day, but she didn't return.

walked the pages to the office. It had closed. He took the scene
home with him and typed it there.

In the morning Izzy showed the new scene to his wife, Barbara,
who had written novels under the name Barbara Bentley. She
read the typescript. She thought the last line was weak. Where
was the payoff for the outrageous revelation? She didn't like it.

"That's what Billy thinks, too," said Izzy. "You're both wrong."

"No."

"Yes," said Izzy. "Audiences think they're smart enough to see a punch line coming. They love to anticipate a joke. In this case, everybody—even the dumbest member of the audience—knows that Jerry has to take off his wig and admit he's a man. They're holding onto their seats because Osgood's going to explode. So. What if there's no explosion? What if there's an understated reaction? Look. We've set up the laugh. It's in the structure of the scene. That work's done. The actual line doesn't matter, as long as it's flat. In fact, the flatter, the better."

The scene went to the studio, where it was mimeographed and distributed. Billy thought about the last line all week. He wasn't the only one.

Marilyn looked at the scene and saw one thing. The last shot was of two men. It wasn't of her. That did it. After her work with me on the process stage Thursday, she walked to her dressing room. There was one more shot to do, but she was not going to act in it if the movie didn't end with a close-up of her. She packed up, gathered her entourage around her, and drove through the Goldwyn gates.

When Billy heard the news, he called Marilyn's stand-in. Then he and Izzy modified the scene. On Friday morning he shot it. The stand-in was sitting with me in the backseat of the motor launch. Billy had me lean over her, obscuring her face. Joe E. Brown and Jack Lemmon were in the front seat. Billy had Joe E. say, "Nobody's perfect."

"Cut." Billy still wasn't sure, but he couldn't think of anything better. "Print it."

Part VI

The Previews

31

On Saturday, November 8, I went with Janet to see Sammy Davis Jr. in a play called *The Desperate Hours*. Janet was eight months along, but she was willing to go to this theater-in-the-round presentation. I'd seen a lot of Sammy at the Goldwyn Studio, since he was playing Sportin' Life in *Porgy and Bess*.

That same night, Marilyn was rushed from the Bel Air Hotel to Cedars of Lebanon Hospital. She thought she was having a miscarriage, but she wasn't. She was kept there for about a week. She was worried that the sleeping pills were going to kill her baby, so she tried to wean herself from them.

On Monday, November 10, Jack and I reported to Stage 4 at Goldwyn for the final scenes of *Some Like It Hot*. We worked for two days, mostly in the lobby and in the third-floor hallway set. Our last setups were in George Raft's hotel room on the afternoon of November 11. The very last lines we said had to do with changing out of drag and getting out of there alive. No kidding! That was exactly how we felt. We'd been in drag since August 4— seventy-three days of shooting. And now no more wigs. No more falsies. No more fucking high heels. Elation. And then—a drop.

I always have a curious feeling when I finish shooting a film. A drop in energy. A lull. A "postpartum" depression. I've been seeing the same faces, hearing the same voices, sharing the same experiences. Suddenly I'm cut off from these people. I turn to make a comment to Jack Lemmon because I know he'll get a kick out of it. He's not there. Where is he? He's gone on to the next thing. Where's Billy Wilder? He's in the editing room with Doane Harrison and Arthur Schmidt. What about Harold Mirisch, whose greeting on Beverly Drive started the whole thing?

Harold was in the field with Arthur Jacobs, trying to put on a brave face. Lloyd Shearer was back, asking pointed questions. "Is Marilyn really worth all the time and trouble she caused you?" How do you answer an impertinent question like that? Harold was honest.

"This is a funny, a riotous picture," said Harold. "Marilyn is marvelous in it. But, yes, her illnesses may have cost us two weeks. Three months is a long shooting schedule for a comedy. It was budgeted at $2.3 million. We've gone about $500,000 over. Which means that we'll need to gross $7 million to break even. I hope we'll make a great deal more. But, to answer your question. Just how much Marilyn is worth in time, trouble and money? We'll have to wait until the picture is released to find that out."

Shearer's article ended with a quote that was attributed to an actor in the film. I didn't give it. I'm sure that Jack didn't. I can't imagine George Raft giving it. But there it was. "Marilyn is a dear, sweet, sincere, adorable girl," said the unnamed actor. "I hope she settles down with Arthur Miller and has a half dozen children. I know she has made a wonderful wife, and she will make an even more wonderful mother. But a great actress she ain't."

Looking back on the period that followed the filming, I don't remember a lull. That would have been nicer than what we had. Billy was struggling with the cutting. His challenge was to find a take in which Marilyn was firing on all pistons and in which Jack and I didn't look pooped. Imagine watching eighty-one takes of "Where's that bourbon?"

I hadn't seen my family in a while. My father and mother had come to the set in August, but that was about it. Late on the night of Sunday, November 16, I got a call from my brother, Robert. He was living with my folks on South Reeves Drive in Beverly Hills. "Daddy has gone to sleep," he said. I bolted to the car. When I got to their house, I found my father lying on the floor. He'd had a heart attack. We lost him. He was just fifty-eight. For the next two days my family and I sat shivah for him. The funeral was on Wednesday. I was in a daze. Then, on Friday, Janet went into labor. I rushed her to Cedars of Lebanon Hospital. On Saturday morning our daughter Jamie Lee was born.

No, I did not see Marilyn at the hospital. She was on her way to New York with Arthur Miller.

While I was coping with real life, Billy was immersed in reel life. I didn't find out until later, but he thought my Josephine voice had recorded too low; the other characters would have been suspicious of me. So he hired Paul Frees, who was a wonderfully versatile actor with an amazing variety of voices, and he dubbed all the lines I'd spoken in falsetto. As if that wasn't enough, Paul also dubbed a couple of lines for Tito Vuolo, the funeral director. Billy didn't like Tito's voice. It sounded too New York and not enough Chicago, I guess.

Billy reached back to his Berlin days for our musical score. Matty Malneck was the Whiteman band member who'd helped Billy communicate with the maestro in 1926. In the thirties Malneck was also writing hit songs. He cowrote "I'm Through with Love," and "Park Avenue Fantasy," which became "Stairway to the Stars." Later he composed for movies. He scored *Witness for the Prosecution*. His music was a natural choice for *Some Like It Hot*. When Adolph Deutsch scored the film, he used "Stairway to the Stars" as Sugar's motif, and Marilyn sang "I'm Through with Love" in the last musical number. Even though Matty's songs came from the thirties, no one complained.

Matty collaborated with Izzy Diamond on a title song for *Some Like It Hot*. Marilyn had not recorded it when she left for New York, so Matty flew there to coach her and get the song recorded. He found her quite cooperative, but for whatever reason the song was never used. While Matty was in New York, he and Marilyn had occasion to go to a restaurant. Sitting in the bar, Matty diplomatically suggested that Marilyn and Billy might mend fences. He thought that their feud was silly. He had an idea. The bartender brought a phone to the bar. Matty dialed Billy's home number and handed the receiver to Marilyn. Audrey Wilder answered in Westwood.

"Hello?"

"Audrey? This is Marilyn."

"Well, hi, Marilyn."

"Is Billy there?"

This photo captures the feeling that Jack and I had when we finished *Some Like It Hot*. We'd worked seventy-three days, from August 4 through November 11, 1958. We felt we'd done a good job, but we had no idea of the stature this movie would attain.

"No, he's not home yet. It's four thirty here, you know."

"Oh. Well, when you see him, will you give him a message for me?"

"Of course, Marilyn."

"Tell him to go fuck himself."

Silence.

"And my warmest personal regards to you, Audrey." Click.

I never heard what Billy said when he got home and heard Marilyn's message. I know that both he and Izzy were disgusted by the way Marilyn treated people whom she considered underlings, people who couldn't fight back. Cursing out an assistant director was one thing. Insulting Billy's wife was another. Marilyn had lit the fuse to a bomb. It wasn't a question of whether it would go off. It was a question of when.

32

On December 16 news came from New York. Marilyn Monroe was in the hospital. She had been rushed there two days earlier. The news did not report that she'd taken Amytal on an empty stomach and—worse—had washed it down with sherry. It did report that she had miscarried. Although she and Arthur Miller knew that this was the result of an ectopic pregnancy, they told no one. On December 18 Miller's mother told Earl Wilson, the gossip columnist at the *New York Post*, that Billy Wilder was responsible for Marilyn's miscarriage. "She had to run upstairs about fourteen times in the picture," said Mrs. Miller. "The temperature in San Diego was about 104. All the time she was not feeling well."

As I said, the temperature when we shot on the pier was around eighty. I didn't see Marilyn do anything so strenuous that it would cause her to miscarry six weeks later. But that's how legends are made, by prevarication. To tell you the truth, I didn't care who caused the miscarriage. All that I cared about was that Marilyn's child had died. I believed the child was mine.

I had been contemplating what I would do when the child was born. I'd heard the stories about Clark Gable and Loretta Young, and how he handled a similar situation. Young was not married and, being Catholic, would not consider an abortion. She went to Europe to have Gable's baby. Ten years or so later, Gable visited Young and met the little girl, whose name was Judy. He never told her he was her father, since she was being raised by Loretta's husband, Tom Lewis. I thought this was sad. I did not relish the idea of my child being raised by Arthur Miller. I hoped that Marilyn and I could work something out. The miscarriage ended that hope.

Coming on the heels of my father's death, the news of the miscarriage hit me hard. It caused me to sink into a depression. It didn't matter that I had two healthy children. It didn't matter that in ten years I'd come from a $75-a-week contract player to a $1-million-a-year star. It didn't matter that I'd just made one of the greatest films of my career or anyone else's. I was deeply depressed. I stopped following the progress of *Some Like It Hot*.

Billy was pushing for a March release. This meant previewing our picture in January. That way there'd still be time for changes. He was happy with the first cut of the film, but one scene bothered him, the one that ends the train sequence. This is the scene where I shake Jack "like a terrier shaking a rat." Jack says, "You wouldn't hit a girl, would you?" Fade out.

Billy wondered if this little scene spoiled the effect of the previous one, where the girls tumble out of the berth. Our scene was cute, but coming where it did, it looked tacked on. The train sequence was super. Maybe it didn't need anything after the party scene. And yet, Billy liked this scene for what it said about the friendship. Izzy didn't feel strongly one way or the other. He couldn't see fretting over it. Let the preview decide. Billy disagreed.

"If it gets laughs," said Billy, "I might be tempted to keep it in. No, Iz. We don't need it." As Billy prepared to cut the scene, he got a call. The production company had lined up a theater for the first sneak preview, but two weeks earlier than Billy had planned. Cutting the scene would mean that he'd have to edit, rescore, and remix an entire reel. There wasn't time.

In September Billy had told the press how funny he thought the film already was. "I may be the first to put English subtitles on an English-speaking movie," he said. "Audiences will be laughing so hard that they won't hear half of the dialogue." He admitted that the premise was a bold one. "I think audiences are ready for it. Movies should be like amusement parks. People should go to them to have fun. There's nothing but fun in our picture. It will be a film I won't be worried about showing, either in the sticks or at the Cannes Film Festival."

The preview took place on Wednesday, January 28, 1959, at the Bay Theatre in Pacific Palisades, a bedroom community on the coast. Billy and Audrey attended, along with Jack and Felicia, Izzy and Barbara, and a number of Mirisch Company executives. Steve Allen was there. So was Joseph Mankiewicz. A lot was riding on this. The film had run up a negative cost of $2,883,848.

There was a sign outside the theater that read "Major Studio Preview Tonight." Apparently the theater's eight hundred patrons didn't realize that. Most of them thought they were going to see Elizabeth Taylor in *Cat on a Hot Tin Roof*. The crowd was typical Pacific Palisades, affluent and older. There were some families, too, which was odd, considering the Taylor film. Maybe they had come for the sneak preview.

The lights dimmed. The credits rolled. If Billy had forgotten David Selznick's prediction, he remembered it then. "Other than the musical score," said Barbara Diamond, "there was nothing in the first few minutes of the film to tip off the audience that this was a comedy. There was a gangster car chase, a speakeasy behind a funeral parlor, and a police raid." The audience sat there, taking the film very seriously. "That audience was skewed very old," said Barbara. "These people weren't ready to laugh. They'd come to see Liz Taylor." Twenty minutes into the film, they hadn't even seen Marilyn Monroe. Then Jack and I showed up in drag. "Children were hauled out of there by their parents," said Jack. "They were muttering, 'Now this is disgusting. What the hell is this?'" The rest of the audience sat with their arms folded.

"Those that didn't walk out sat in deathly silence," said Barbara.

"Nobody laughed except for a couple of our friends," said Audrey.

"It was unequivocally the worst preview of any film I have ever been in," said Jack.

"The worst preview in history," said Barbara.

After the film ended, Audrey nudged Billy. "Go mix with the crowd," she told him. "Hear what they're saying." Billy went to the lobby. Audience members were filling out preview cards. "They didn't know whether it was okay to laugh or not," recalled Audrey. "They just didn't know what to do." Billy shook Steve Allen's hand. Most of the guffaws had come from him. Joe Mankiewicz came up behind Billy, put his hand on his shoulder, and tried to reassure him. "It's all right, Billy," he said. "It happens to all of us."

The Mirisch brothers took Billy aside. "They started telling him what he had to do," said Jack. "All that bullshit that heads of companies try to tell directors. Cut this. Cut that. Show more Marilyn." The Mirisches had more advice. "You cannot have a farce or a comedy, whatever this is, that's running two hours," said one. "It can't be done. You can't go more than an hour and thirty-five minutes."

"Right," nodded Billy. "Okay. Fine. Tomorrow Iz and I will start working on it."

Jack was concerned. He called Billy a couple of days later. Billy had just emerged from the editing room.

"I made the cut," he told Jack.

"You made the what?"

"Cut. Not 'cuts.'"

"What did you cut?"

"The scene where you crawl up into Tony's berth. The last scene in the train. That's no longer there."

Billy explained that he'd managed to book a preview that night. It was at the Village Theatre in Westwood. So he cut the scene right out of the first answer print and hot spliced the ends together. There was no time to do anything else.

"The Village had a much more sophisticated audience," said Jack. "College kids, older people, young people, everything."

Billy had an idea. He put a sign up. It read, "Minor Studio Preview Tonight." This time the audience was in on the joke.

"This was a hip crowd," said Audrey. "They laughed. And laughed. You couldn't hear the dialogue."

The first scene of Jack and me got so many laughs that they missed the line about "Jell-O on springs." And our scene with the maracas caused hysteria. "This was a scene of about two minutes," said Billy, "but it was the biggest sustained laugh I had in any of my pictures."

"The entire audience was screaming," said Jack. "It was an enormous success."

Part VII

The Press

33

After the triumphant preview in Westwood, Billy Wilder added a few more angles of Jack Lemmon and me at the train station and a couple more angles of Jack with the maracas. This was to allow time for laughs. Then he sent our movie to the big city—and with it, an invitation to Marilyn Monroe.

On February 5, 1959, she attended the New York Press Association preview. It was being held at the Loew's Lexington Theatre, which was at that time located at 571 Lexington Avenue. Marilyn wore a new upswept hairdo, chandelier earrings, and a white silk gown. Accompanied by a tuxedoed Arthur Miller, she was stunning. "Monroe and Miller were literally mobbed by fans as they arrived," recalled writer Warren G. Harris. "Once they'd been escorted safely inside the theater, the other patrons were considerate and left them alone. This was a huge theater. There was a capacity audience that night. *Some Like It Hot* nearly brought down the house with laughter."

After the film was over, police escorted Monroe and Miller out. Montgomery Clift was there, hoping to get a ride with them. He was caught in the uproar and pushed along the side of the limousine. He pounded on the roof, but they didn't know it was him. They took off without him.

The *Variety* review was as friendly as we'd hoped; maybe more so:

> *Some Like It Hot*, directed in masterly style by Billy Wilder, is probably the funniest picture of recent memory. It's a whacky, clever, farcical comedy that starts off like a firecracker and keeps on throwing off lively sparks till the very end. Pictures like this, with a sense of humor that is as broad

as it is sophisticated, come along only infrequently. . . . Even so, the film has its faults. It's too long, for one, being a small joke milked like a dairy; one or two scenes skirt the limits of good taste. But who'll care?

After fifty years, it's still exciting to read *Variety*'s description of how the audience reacted.

> Tony Curtis and Jack Lemmon walking down the station platform dressed as girls, swinging their hips, bring the house down.
>
> The audience virtually explodes when, after being grabbed by Curtis in his bosomy disguise, Lemmon announces angrily: "I lost one of my chests!"
>
> Marilyn's a comedienne with that combination of sex appeal and timing that just can't be beat. If, at the time of the filming she was pregnant, and her tight dresses don't fit very well, never mind.
>
> Alternating shots of Miss Monroe trying to stimulate Curtis on a couch, while Lemmon and Joe E. Brown live it up on the dance floor, rate as a classic sequence.
>
> It's obvious that Tony Curtis enjoys the part of a comedian, and he makes the most of it.

I was delighted to read this review. Marilyn was not. Back at her apartment, she and Miller compared impressions. He thought the film was excellent and that it proved her a skilled comedienne. She did not. "I don't want to be funny," cried Marilyn. "Everybody's going to laugh at me. And not because of my acting. Because of how I look. I look like a fat pig. Those goddamned cocksuckers made me look like a funny fat pig!"

At this point Billy felt it was time to clear the air. On February 10 the *New York Herald Tribune* published a few choice words. Billy said that his health had improved since he'd finished directing Marilyn. "I am eating better," said Billy. "My back doesn't ache any more. I am able to sleep for the first time in months. And I can look at my wife without wanting to hit her because she's a woman. Would I direct Marilyn again? I have discussed this with my doctor and my psychiatrist and my accountant. They tell me that I'm too old and too rich to go through it again." I guess he'd been pushed too far. The man was an artist. He had an ego. It was bruised. And his spouse had been insulted.

When Marilyn read the article, she called Earl Wilson. "Who says stars are temperamental?" she asked. "Now it's directors who get that way!" Wilson oozed with sympathy as he wrote, "Marilyn wishes that Billy would remember that *Some Like It Hot* cost her the baby."

A telegram arrived at Billy's office a day later. It was from Arthur Miller. It read:

> I cannot let your vicious attack on Marilyn go unchallenged. You were officially informed by Marilyn's physician that due to her pregnancy she was not able to work a full day. You chose to ignore this fact during the making of the picture. . . . She went on with the picture out of a sense of responsibility not only to herself but to you and the cast and producer. Twelve hours after the last shooting day her miscarriage began. . . . [She] began this picture with a throat infection so serious that a specialist forbade her to work at all until it was cured. She went on nevertheless. Your jokes, Billy, are not quite hilarious enough to conceal the fact [that] you are an unjust man and a cruel one. My only solace is that despite you, her beauty and her humanity shine through as they always have.

Miller's claims about Marilyn's health were unfounded. After all, a woman can have only one miscarriage in a pregnancy. And it had been duly reported in December. Not November. And certainly not twelve hours after Marilyn left the set. I never saw the slightest evidence of a "throat infection," unless that thermos contained cough medicine. Amazing how a sane man could be pulled into his wife's craziness. Billy responded:

> I am deeply sorry that she lost her baby but I must reject the implication that overwork or inconsiderate treatment by me or anyone else associated with the production was

in any way responsible for it. The fact is that the company pampered her, coddled her, and acceded to all her whims. The only one who showed any lack of consideration was Marilyn, in her treatment of her costars and her coworkers right from the first day. Before there was any hint of pregnancy, her chronic tardiness and unpreparedness cost us eighteen shooting days, hundreds of thousands of dollars, and countless heartaches. This having been my second picture with Marilyn, I understand her problems. Her biggest problem is that she doesn't understand anybody else's problems. If you took a quick poll among the cast and crew on the subject of Marilyn you would find a positively overwhelming lack of popularity. Had you, dear Arthur, been not her husband, but her writer and director, and been subjected to all the indignities I was, you would have thrown her out on her can, thermos bottle and all, to avoid a nervous breakdown. I did the braver thing. I had a nervous breakdown.

Meanwhile, another pronouncement made its way into the press. "The question is whether Marilyn is a person at all," said Billy. "Perhaps she is one of the greatest DuPont products ever invented. She has breasts like granite. She defies gravity. She has a brain full of holes, like Swiss cheese. She hasn't the vaguest conception of the time of day. She arrives late and tells you she couldn't find the studio when she's been working there for years." As we knew, she'd only been working there a month when she said that, but he made his point. Miller was determined to have the last word. He sent another telegram. It read:

That others would have attacked Marilyn is hardly a justification for you to have done so yourself. The simple truth is that, whatever the circumstances, she did her job and did it superbly, while your published remarks create the contrary impression without any mitigation. That is what is unfair. She is not the first actress who must follow her own path to a performance. Given her evident excellence it was your job as director not to reject her approach because it was unfamiliar to you but in the light of the results you could see every day on the screen, you should have realized that her way to working was valid for her, completely serious and not a self indulgence. . . . She was not there to demonstrate how obedient she could be but how excellent in performance. That you lost sight of this is your failure and the basic reason for my protest at the injustice not only toward her as my wife but as the kind of artist one does not come on every day in the week. After all, she has created something extraordinary, and it is simply improper for you of all people to mock it.

But Billy was not one to submit to moral indignation. He fired back.

In order to hasten the burial of the hatchet, I hereby acknowledge that good wife Marilyn is a unique personality and I am the Beast of Belsen. But in the immortal words of Joe E. Brown, "Nobody is perfect."

34

In March 1959 *Some Like It Hot* was "on the launching pad," as we used to say in those early days of the Space Race. There was a lot of anticipation and a lot at stake: not just $2.8 million, but the careers of a lot of major players. So when Billy Wilder submitted his final cut to the Production Code Administration, he did so with a bit of apprehension.

The PCA was run by an enlightened chap named Geoffrey Shurlock. His job (paid by the industry) was to censor our movies so that no one else would want to. In the old days there'd been eight censor boards. They used to cut the hell out of movies they thought would offend people. Now there were only four remaining boards. The PCA put a stop to the butchery of film prints, but it also hamstrung artists who wanted to use adult terms to tell adult stories. Billy was supposed to submit his scripts to the PCA before shooting. He stopped doing that when the PCA rejected his script of *The Bad Seed* and then okayed Mervyn LeRoy's. There was some history between Billy and Geoff, so it came as a surprise when Geoff approved the finished print of *Some Like It Hot* and congratulated Billy on its excellence. Not everyone agreed.

The PCA had been instituted in 1934 after a grassroots campaign against "immoral movies" by the National Catholic Legion of Decency. The Legion told Roman Catholics what films they could or could not see using a ratings system to classify them: A was morally unobjectionable; D was objectionable in part, C was condemned. In 1957 the Legion expanded its A rating to include A-I, morally unobjectionable for general patronage; A-II, morally unobjectionable for adults and adolescents; and A-III, morally unobjectionable for adults. On March 5 Geoff received a letter from the Very Reverend Monsignor Thomas F. Little, S. T. L., who was the executive secretary of the Legion:

> *Some Like It Hot*, though it purports to be a comedy, contains screen material elements that are judged to be seriously offensive to Christian and traditional standards of morality and decency, including gross suggestiveness in costuming, dialogue, and situations. Since the initiation of the triple-A method of classifying films in December 1957, this film has given the Legion the greatest cause for concern in its evaluation of Code Seal pictures. The subject matter of transvestism naturally leads to complications; in this film there seemed to us clear inference of homosexuality and lesbianism. The dialogue was not only double entendre but also outright smut. The offense in costuming was obvious.

Geoff defended the film. "So far," he responded, "there is simply no adverse reaction at all; nothing but praise for it as a hilariously funny movie. I am not suggesting, of course, that there are not dangers connected with a story of this type. But girls dressed as men, and occasionally men dressed as women for proper plot purposes, has been standard theatrical fare as far back as *As You Like It* and *Twelfth Night*." He could not defend the "exaggerated costumes" worn by Marilyn, but he felt that the film was essentially good-natured and consequently harmless.

Monsignor Little felt otherwise. He gave *Some Like It Hot* a B rating, saying that it was "morally objectionable in part for all." The Catholic population was clustered in cities that had the big movie palaces, but many Catholics thought the Legion's classification was silly. This made the news and influenced two of the remaining censor boards. The Kansas Censor Board demanded that United Artists cut one hundred feet of our love scene in the yacht. UA refused, having won a similar battle four years earlier over Otto Preminger's *The Moon Is Blue*. Kansas would not back down. Our film would not play there, it seemed. Then the Tennessee censors got into the act and refused to let minors see the film. This generated welcome publicity for UA, the Mirisches, and Billy.

Publicity was also being generated by Marilyn Monroe. On March 18 she appeared at a press luncheon at the Ambassador East in Chicago, a setting that was in keeping with the film's gangland theme. A fretful photographer spilled a drink on her, but she kept her composure. She affected guys that way. Something Freudian about it.

The world premiere of *Some Like It Hot* was planned for March 29 at the Loew's State Theatre. The New York movie palace located at 1540 Broadway was reopening after a year of "modernization." This was funny. A 1920s comedy should have premiered in a house that looked like 1921. Unfortunately, I couldn't be there, but I received letters from fans, and I have one that captures all the excitement of that night.

George Zeno was fourteen when his father took him to Loew's State on March 29, 1959. He later wrote:

> The premiere happened on a very, very cold night. My father and I waited about two hours for Marilyn to show

up. By this time there were more than a thousand people milling around. They were all around the theatre and across Seventh Avenue. There was a major traffic jam. The whole Times Square area was clogged. Part of that was due to the number of celebrities arriving. We saw Celeste Holm, George Raft, Harry Belafonte, and Gloria Swanson.

The minute Marilyn arrived, the crowd went mad. There was total confusion. People were pushing, shoving, screaming. Barricades were knocked down. I saw my father get pushed. He fell. I hesitated for a split second, wondering what to do. Help my father? Or get close to the woman I'd idolized for six years? My father wasn't hurt. As he was getting up and brushing himself off, Marilyn got out of her limousine.

We'd been pushed close to it, so I got a look I'll never forget. Marilyn was that "vision in white" you hear about, but *real*. White fur. Silver white gown. Platinum white hair. Porcelain white skin. All I could do was stare. She seemed more like an apparition than a flesh-and-blood person, but that apparition was burned into my memory. She waved and smiled at everyone. Then they rushed her into the theater before anything could happen to her. Like me, everyone was a little stunned.

And that movie! The laughter was so loud that my ears were still ringing the next morning. After the event, I knew that this movie was going to be Marilyn's biggest hit, the greatest comedy ever. For a cold night, this was the kind of hot that people wanted.

A. H. Weiler's review appeared in the *New York Times* the next day. To read it, you would have thought that watching us was like taking medicine. "Let's face it," wrote Mr. Weiler. "Two hours is too long to harp on one joke. But Billy Wilder . . . proves that he is as professional as anyone in Hollywood. Abetted by such equally proficient operatives as Marilyn Monroe, Jack Lemmon, and Tony Curtis, he surprisingly has developed a completely unbelievable plot into a broad farce in which authentically comic action vies with snappy and sophisticated dialogue." Yes, but did you like it? "*Some Like It Hot* does cool off considerably now and again, but Mr. Wilder and his carefree clowns keep it crackling and funny most of the time."

The Hollywood premiere took place on April 8 at Grauman's Chinese Theatre. The *Los Angeles Times* review was, if possible, even less kind. Philip Scheuer, you'll recall, was a visitor to our set more than once. It was with disbelief that we read the title of his review. "*Some Like It Hot* Not as Hot as Expected." What?

"*Some Like It Hot* is often funny," wrote Scheuer, "but is not the unalloyed delight it was cracked up to be. Considering that Billy Wilder is a veteran comedy constructionist, I was rather surprised to discover that it is not at all sure what kind of comedy it is. No doubt can exist, however, that it is primarily a sex farce." Scheuer found the gangster bits "questionably macabre," the yacht scene "baldly suggestive," Marilyn "provocative" but not looking or playing her best. He found Joe E. Brown's curtain line "a startler from one who for years has eschewed anything blue." The astute Mr. Scheuer saved his only coherent English for me. "Curtis is good enough . . . but his Cary Grant accent (not his doing) annoyed the hell out of me."

Some actors never read reviews. I do. Mr. Scheuer's review annoyed the hell out of *me*. To make myself feel better, I bought the rights to the autobiography of the Italian poet Gabriele d'Annunzio, a wild, sexy artist not unlike myself.

Part VIII

The Public

35

At the end of the first week of our movie's release, Walter Mirisch was worried. The grosses were not so good. Apparently the potential audience members had read the reviews and were adopting the proverbial wait-and-see stance. We held our breath. At the end of the second week, grosses were twice the first week's. And at the end of the third week, they were even higher. Izzy Diamond later described this as "one of those rare phenomena in the picture business—it just kept building." *Some Like It Hot* stayed at Grauman's for nine weeks, which was almost unheard of. Equally amazing was its return to a first-run theater on Broadway within weeks of its record-breaking first run. Interestingly enough, in a year dominated by talk of epics and dramas—*Ben-Hur, Compulsion*, and *The Long, Hot Summer*—the hits included comedies. The highest-grossing comedy ($12.3 million) was *The Shaggy Dog*. The next ($9.3 million) was *Auntie Mame*. Then came *Some Like It Hot*, with domestic rentals of $7.5 million and foreign rentals of $5.25 million. Its unusual release pattern quickly moved it ahead of the other films, and reissues kept it there. Add television, repertory, video, laser disc, cable, and DVD, and you have a film that may have earned as much as $30 million in fifty years' time.

We were honored to be nominated in so many categories of Academy Awards. There were six: Jack Lemmon for Best Actor; Billy Wilder for Best Director; Billy Wilder and I. A. L. Diamond for Best Adapted Screenplay; Charles Lang for Best Cinematography; Ted Haworth and Edward G. Boyle for Best Art Direction; and George Orry-Kelly for Best Costume Design.

Of these, the only winner was Orry-Kelly. We might have had a
chance if it wasn't for *Ben-Hur*. The only other recognition came
from the Writers Guild, which gave Billy and Izzy the award for
the Best Written American Comedy of 1959.

The only other recognition? What am I saying? *Some Like It
Hot* may be the most profitable comedy in the history of motion
pictures. Certainly the most beloved. With affection like that, who
needs recognition?

To give you an idea of the love this picture has engendered,
I can tell you about the Moscow International Film Festival in
1963. I'd gotten invited, so I called United Artists, and the next
morning I was carrying two cans of film with me onto a plane.
When I got to Moscow, I was taken to a huge auditorium—like a
gymnasium—with folding chairs. That was the "theater." At one
end of this big room was a platform made of wood suspended
between two ladders, and on that were two ancient projectors.
The festival people asked me where I wanted to stand and intro-
duce the film.

"I'll go up there on one of those ladders so the people can
see me." So I climbed up this rickety ladder, all the way up, with
nothing underneath me, and hung on and talked to this crowd of
maybe two thousand people. There was a translator, of course.
They were all looking up at me. I told them what the picture was
about. And I talked about Marilyn and me. And, oh, they went
wild. They loved me. But that was nothing compared to what they
did when the movie came on.

The same man was translating the dialogue into Russian
through a microphone. And that crowd caught every nuance of
the movie. When he translated the very last line of dialogue—
"Nobody's perfect"—the place fell apart. They screamed. They
carried on. It was absolute madness. They loved it. And I loved it.
Let me tell you, I *loved* it.

Epilogue

Epilogue

Fifty years have passed since *Some Like It Hot* was created. I say *created* because it was—it is—a work of art. I'm eighty-four now. I live in Las Vegas. I create art. I paint. I spend time with my wife, Jill. We save racehorses that are in danger of being exterminated. We rescue them and give them a sanctuary. It gives us a feeling of contributing something. You might ask if I feel that my movies contributed to our culture. I do. As I said before, people talk to me about this film or that film, people who are too young to have seen the film when it came out, and I marvel at the power of film. If I had gone from *Golden Boy* to Broadway, the performances I would have given—where would they be now?

I feel fortunate to have worked in motion pictures. Something I created fifty years ago is bringing pleasure to someone I can't see and may never meet. It's hard not to feel good about something so transcendent. Although, I'll tell you, when I recall those Hollywood parties, none of us was thinking about posterity. We never thought that anyone would want to look at our current film a month after it came out, much less fifty years later. All we cared about was success. A better role. A better contract. A better percentage. Success.

What does success mean in Hollywood? Power—the power to choose. *Some Like It Hot* gave me the power to choose the costar of my next film. I had idolized Cary Grant since I was a teenager. Thanks to the film I'd just done, I got to make a film with Cary.

Billy told me that he ran *Some Like It Hot* for Cary so he could see my impression of him. When it was over, Cary said, "I don't talk like that." Come on, Cary. Of course you did.

But Cary loved me for that. It was my way of bringing him and Billy together. They'd always wanted to work together, but it had never happened. When one was free, the other was busy, and so forth. They were frustrated about it. So when I played Cary in *Some Like It Hot*, it was like Billy finally got to direct Cary. And then I got Cary to work with me in *Operation Petticoat*. And that was satisfying—being on a submarine with my idol, almost twenty years after I'd seen him in *Destination Tokyo* and joined the navy in emulation.

After *Some Like It Hot* became a steamrolling hit, I was a major player. But I didn't realize it. I had made it really big and didn't know it. Well, I kind of saw it. And I gradually realized it, but I didn't understand how I got there. I looked at the film and I thought that in the beginning of it I was weaker than I really was. Everything was done to keep Marilyn happy. She was chosen, favored over Jack and me. That's what colored my perception of the film for a long time. Too long. But I finally got past that.

I thought a lot about Marilyn in the years after we made *Some Like It Hot*. I felt like things were unresolved between us. I saw her trying to pull herself together, to make a go of her marriage, and to be acknowledged for her talent. I also saw her becoming spoiled, slovenly, deluded, and addicted. It got to be a very sad spectacle. I remember the last time I saw her. It was at Peter Lawford's. I was hanging out with Frank Sinatra and his Rat Pack at that time. So there was the occasional trip to Lawford's beach house. Marilyn was there one day. She looked tired and unhappy. But her eyes lit up when she saw me across the room. I went over to her.

"Where's your green convertible?" she asked me.

"You mean the one with the Dynaflow Drive?"

"I guess so," she smiled, a little vaguely. "Yeah. Uh huh. That one."

"In Buick heaven."

"That's nice."

I squeezed her hand and excused myself. And that was the last I saw of her.

Sad? Yeah. The slump she went into in the summer of sixty-two was even sadder. I'd heard about her problems with Twentieth. I had my own problems at that point. I was being divorced by Janet and getting ready to leave the country. I wasn't able to reach out to Marilyn. I was in Europe when she died. I think about her. I wonder if she's found peace. If she knows—or cares—how much she's loved. And how fondly I remember her. I hope she knows that.

And Jack Lemmon, how much joy he still brings to people. Whenever that funny close-up of him in *Some Like It Hot* hits the screen. And that insane giggle. Jack and I were a team. Everything we did was to feed each other. Looking back on it now, I realize that we switched roles as the film progressed. First I was the straight man and he was the comic. In another scene, he'd be straight man and I'd be carrying on. Sometimes our roles would flip-flop during a scene. We had to be flexible and inventive. It wasn't complicated particularly, but we had to be attuned to what it was.

And you know what we were doing? We were playing Billy Wilder and Izzy Diamond. Don't ask me who was who. It doesn't matter, because they switched characters while they were acting it out and writing it down, too. All I know is that Jack and I were in front of a camera playing versions of Billy and Izzy. You'll probably ask why Billy and Izzy didn't get in front of the camera and play it themselves, like Woody Allen or Mel Brooks. I have no idea. I never asked them. Maybe they were too shy. Who knows?

Years after our picture was finished, I looked at it and realized that it was bigger than all of us put together. Could they have done it with someone else in my part? Or Jack's part? Or Marilyn's part? No. Could someone remake it now? Of course not. Billy and Izzy tailored the characters to us as we were creating them. We had to adjust ourselves to that. It was demanding and trying and sometimes exhausting, but it was worth it. Because of that process, *Some Like It Hot* is truly our movie. It was tailored to our individual talents and to our collective talents. Brilliantly conceived and brilliantly tailored. I should know. My father was a tailor.

NOTES

Chapter 3
16 *"Nothing less than"* Diamond, "The Day Marilyn Needed 47 Takes," p. 135.
17 *"Iz"* Ibid.

Chapter 5
25 *"Do you believe"* Sikov, *On Sunset Boulevard*, p. 28.
26 *"I'm afraid"* Ibid., p. 367.
27 *"She had trouble"* Ibid., p. 367.
27 *"Marilyn wanted the"* Crowe, *Conversations with Wilder*, p. 161.
27 *"When you got her"* Spoto, *Marilyn Monroe*, p. 287.
28 *"As one Arthur"* Letter, Billy Wilder to Marilyn Monroe, March 17, 1958, Billy Wilder Papers, Special Collections, the Fairbanks Center for Motion Picture Study, Beverly Hills.

Chapter 7
38 *"If Marilyn wants to"* Wood, *The Bright Side of Billy Wilder*, p. 158.
39 *"Lee, I've got a real"* Guiles, *Norma Jean*, p. 234.
40 *"Should I do my"* Rosten, *Marilyn*, p. 76.

40 *"Dear Marilyn:"* Telegram, Billy Wilder to Marilyn Monroe, April 25, 1958, BW-FCMPS.

41 *"Mm hm. Okay. Now . . . let's see"* Auiler and Castle, *Some Like It Hot*, p. 238.

41 *"Do me a favor"* Ibid.

42 *"I want this kid"* Ibid.

44 *"This is the guy"* Ibid.

Chapter 8

48 *"I'm working on"* Hopper, "Marilyn Returning to Hollywood."

49 *"Marilyn Monroe gloriously"* Smith, "Marilyn Returns."

51 *"Curtis looks"* Sherman, "Cityside."

51 *"I've been working"* Scheuer, "Billy Wilder Tells Plans for Marilyn."

52 *"She wore"* Sherman, "Cityside."

Chapter 12

75 *"I want the world"* Sikov, *On Sunset Boulevard*, p. 417.

75 *"I am very"* Crowe, *Conversations with Wilder*, p. 63.

76 *"It's like shooting"* Wood, *The Bright Side of Billy Wilder*, p. 19.

Chapter 13

79 *"My hair was"* Scott, "Living Doll."

79 *"No other blonde"* Crowe, *Conversations with Wilder*, p. 165.

79 *"They changed it"* Scott, "Living Doll."

79 *"Billy, you have to"* Sikov, *On Sunset Boulevard*, p. 418.

80 *"Neither my husband"* "Marilyn Sips Champagne to Celebrate."

Chapter 14

90 *"I could watch Marilyn"* Hyams, "Marilyn Is Back!" p. 11.

92 *"You aren't surprised"* Guiles, *Norma Jean*, p. 238.

Chapter 16

97 *"Everything is in such"* Sikov, *On Sunset Boulevard*, p. 418.

106 *"Billy made a closeup"* Widener, *Lemmon*, p. 173.

106 *"He was a great"* Crowe, *Conversations with Wilder*, p. 129.

Chapter 17

109 *"I've asked Marilyn"* Guiles, *Norma Jean*, p. 238

Chapter 19
123 *"Don't give up"* Spoto, *Marilyn Monroe*, p. 402.
124 *"It took me"* Freedland, *Jack Lemmon*, p. 60.

Chapter 20
131 *"She was having"* Auiler and Castle, *Some Like It Hot*, p. 272.
132 *"Billy handed me"* Ibid., p. 421.

Chapter 21
139 *"There were days"* Spoto, *Marilyn Monroe*, p. 405.
143 *"There are very few"* Hyams, "Marilyn Is Back!" p. 11.

Chapter 22
146 *"Now listen, guys"* Auiler and Castle, *Some Like It Hot*, p. 277.
146 *"She'd pick up"* Spoto, *Marilyn Monroe*, p. 405.
146 *"Maybe it's a"* Wood, *The Bright Side of Billy Wilder*, p. 155
150 *"Marilyn was trained"* Ibid., p. 153.
150 *"When I drove"* Auiler and Castle, *Some Like It Hot*, p. 272.
151 *"Marilyn was an excellent"* Crowe, *Conversations with Wilder*, p. 36.
151 *"Marilyn was very"* Scott, "Living Doll."

Chapter 23
155 *"Everybody connected"* Whitcomb, "The New Monroe," p. 71.
157 *"She was very"* Crowe, *Conversations with Wilder*, p. 36.

Chapter 24
159 *"I have never watched"* Whitcomb, "The New Monroe," p. 69.
159 *"Billy had to have"* Auiler and Castle, *Some Like It Hot*, p. 280.
159 *"I never knew"* Leaming, *Marilyn Monroe*, p. 312.
160 *"We were in mid-flight"* Guiles, *Norma Jean*, p. 239.
161 *"Do you have"* Whitcomb, "The New Monroe," p. 70.

Chapter 25
162 *"Marilyn Monroe's closest"* Hopper, "Mitzi Gaynor and Niven Will Costar."
163 *"Paula sympathized"* Guiles, *Norma Jean*, p. 238.
163 *"Here you have"* Leaming, *Marilyn Monroe*, p. 313.
164 *"We could hear Marilyn"* Cerf, "The Late, Late Show-ups."
166 *"What do you think"* Auiler and Castle, *Some Like It Hot*, p. 277.
166 *"Billy, how many"* Leaming, *Marilyn Monroe*, p. 315.
167 *"I swallowed"* Crowe, *Conversations with Wilder*, p. 164.

Chapter 26

167   *"I've been having"*   Auiler and Castle, *Some Like It Hot*, p. 277.

168   *"The whole idea"*   Sikov, *On Sunset Boulevard*, p. 417.

168   *"Monroe demanded"*   Spoto, *Marilyn Monroe*, p. 399.

168   *"My wife is"*   Wood, *The Bright Side of Billy Wilder*, p. 155.

168   *"You're trying"*   Guiles, *Norma Jean*, p. 239.

173   *"Everyone else was"*   Scott, "Living Doll."

174   *"Thank you for"*   Rosten, *Marilyn*, p. 77.

Chapter 27

175   *"I woke up"*   Crowe, *Conversations with Wilder*, p. 37.

176   *"Sugar Kane will"*   Chierichetti, *Hollywood Costume Design*, p. 101.

181   *"Gee! Marilyn"*   "Cast of Characters."

Chapter 28

183   *"Marilyn had a kind"*   Widener, *Lemmon*, p. 170.

Chapter 30

188   *"And Jerry"*   Sikov, *On Sunset Boulevard*, p. 423.

190   *"That's what Billy"*   Auiler and Castle, *Some Like It Hot*, p. 249.

Chapter 31

193   *"Is Marilyn really"*   Shearer, "How Much Time," p. 21.

194   *"Hello?"*   Wood, *The Bright Side of Billy Wilder*, p. 153.

Chapter 32

196   *"She had to run"*   Sikov, *On Sunset Boulevard*, p. 425.

197   *"If it gets laughs"*   Diamond, "The Day Marilyn Needed 47 Takes," p. 136.

198   *"I may be"*   Johnson, "Marilyn Rivaled by 'Dolls'."

198   *"Other than the"*   Auiler and Castle, *Some Like It Hot*, p. 293.

199   *"I made the cut"*   Ibid., p. 295.

Chapter 33

202   *"Monroe and Miller"*   Author interview with Warren G. Harris, May 10, 2009.

202   "Some Like It Hot, *directed"*   "Some Like It Hot," *Variety*, February 6, 1959.

203   *"I don't want to be"*   Leaming, *Marilyn Monroe*, p. 313.

203 *"I am eating"* Wood, *The Bright Side of Billy Wilder*, p. 155.

204 *"Who says stars"* Ibid.

204 *"I cannot let your"* Ibid., p. 158.

205 *"The question is"* Sikov, *On Sunset Boulevard*, p. 425.

205 *"That others would"* Wood, *The Bright Side of Billy Wilder*, p. 160.

Chapter 34

207 "Some Like It Hot, *though it"* Thomas Little, letter to Geoffrey Shurlock, March 5, 1959, *Some Like It Hot* file, in the Production Code Administration papers, MPAA Collection, Margaret Herrick Library, Fairbanks Center for Motion Picture Study (hereinafter PCA).

207 *"So far"* Geoffrey Shurlock, letter to Thomas Little, March 18, 1959, *Some Like It Hot* file, PCA.

BIBLIOGRAPHY

Books

Auiler, Dan, and Alison Castle. *Some Like It Hot*. Berlin: Taschen, 2005.

Chierichetti, David. *Hollywood Costume Design*. New York: Harmony Books, 1976.

Crowe, Cameron. *Conversations with Wilder*. New York: Alfred A. Knopf, 1999.

Curtis, Tony, and Barry Paris. *Tony Curtis: The Autobiography*. New York: William Morrow and Company, 1993.

Curtis, Tony, and Peter Golenbeck. *Tony Curtis: American Prince*. New York: Harmony Books, 2008.

Freedland, Michael. *Jack Lemmon*. New York: St. Martin's Press, 1985.

Greenberg, Joel, and Charles Higham. *The Celluloid Muse: Hollywood Directors Speak*. New York: Signet Books, 1972.

Guiles, Fred Lawrence. *Norma Jean: The Life of Marilyn Monroe*. New York: McGraw-Hill Book Company, 1969.

Leaming, Barbara. *Marilyn Monroe*. London: Weidenfeld and Nicolson, 1998.

Rosten, Norman. *Marilyn: An Untold Story*. New York: Signet Press, 1973.

Sikov, Ed. *On Sunset Boulevard: The Life and Times of Billy Wilder*. New York: Hyperion Press, 1998.

Spoto, Donald. *Marilyn Monroe: The Biography*. New York: HarperCollins Publishers, 1993.

Widener, Don. *Lemmon: A Biography*. New York: MacMillan Publishing Company, 1975.

Wood, Tom. *The Bright Side of Billy Wilder, Primarily*. Garden City, NY: Doubleday and Co., 1968.

Signed Articles

Cerf, Bennett. "The Late, Late Show-ups." *Los Angeles Times*, September 20, 1959, p. J17.

Diamond, I. A. L. "The Day Marilyn Needed 47 Takes to Remember to Say 'Where's the Bourbon?'" *California*, December 1985, pp. 132, 135–36.

Hopper, Hedda. "Marilyn Returning to Hollywood." *Los Angeles Times*, June 22, 1958, p. E3.

———. "Mitzi Gaynor and Niven Will Costar." *Los Angeles Times*, October 20, 1958, p. C10.

Hyams, Joe. "Marilyn Is Back!" *This Week* Magazine, October 5, 1958, pp. 10–11.

———. "Uproar in an Upper Berth." *Los Angeles Times*, January 4, 1959, p. 110.

Johnson, Erskine. "Marilyn Rivaled by 'Dolls'." *Los Angeles Mirror-News*, September 18, 1958, p. 13.

Scheuer, Philip K. "Billy Wilder Tells Plans for Marilyn." *Los Angeles Times*, July 10, 1958, p. B9.

Scott, Vernon. "Living Doll: Marilyn Monroe's Dawdling Makes Money for Cast." *New York Daily News*, December 20, 1958.

Shearer, Lloyd. "How Much Time and Trouble Is Marilyn Monroe Worth?" *Parade*, December 7, 1958, pp. 20–21.

Sherman, Gene. "Cityside." *Los Angeles Times*, July 10, 1958, p. 2.

Smith, Jack. "Marilyn Returns." *Los Angeles Times*, July 9, 1958, p. 3.

Whitcomb, Jon. "The New Monroe." *Cosmopolitan*, March 1959, pp. 68–71.

Unsigned Articles

"Cast of Characters." *Time*, November 17, 1958, p. 74.

"Marilyn Sips Champagne to Celebrate." *Los Angeles Times*, August 8, 1958, pp. 2, 16.

INDEX

Page references in *italics* refer to illustrations.